INSPIRE YOURSELF

by

VERNON HOWARD

NEW LIFE FOUNDATION
Pine, Arizona 85544

Fifth Printing 1994
Copyright 1975 by Vernon Howard

ISBN 0-911203-26-5
Library of Congress Catalog Card Number 74-28713

FOR INFORMATION ON CLASSES, BOOKS,
TAPES AND VIDEO CASSETTES, WRITE:
NEW LIFE
PO BOX 2230
PINE, ARIZONA 85544

CONTENTS

AN INVITATION TO LET THIS BOOK
CHANGE YOUR LIFE

This book contains hundreds of stories and teachings aimed at one target—a completely new life for you. This is a unique teaching technique and an inspiring way to become the victorious person you want to be. While the stories are certainly interesting, they contain much more than mere entertainment. Each story includes several fundamental facts by which anyone can obtain riches he never dreamed existed.

Many stories are case-histories of men and women who have found themselves at last. For example, STORMY WEATHER shows how Eva rightly solved the problem of a broken romance. In SOMETHING TO THINK ABOUT, Lowell learned how to avoid the traps of deceptive people.

If some of these ideas seem strange at first, that is superb. Why? Because it means you are sighting entirely new guideposts which will lead you up the right paths. Have no dismay if you do not understand these teachings at first. They are not too hard to grasp. Other people have understood them, winning life-refreshment, and so can you. Just remember that whatever is necessary for you is also possible for you. Be of good cheer, for life is on your side.

The term *esoterics* refers to all these truly accurate teachings by which anyone can attain a new mind and a new life. Esotericism is a science just as practical as astonomy or chemistry.

For maximum benefit, use this book as follows: 1. Remember the power of receptivity. To be receptive means to set aside acquired beliefs and opinions to permit entrance of the new and the relaxing. Whoever daringly ventures out of *his* harbor will happily enter *the* Harbor. 2. The single sentence following each story is just one of the many guides in the story, so try to see a new lesson with every review. Fresh knowledge is there all right, ready to reveal itself to an alert mind. It is like a gold mine exposing new nuggets every hour. 3. Join with other interested people in classes and group discussions. The *Vernon Howard Study Groups* have helped many seekers.

These guides extend a friendly welcome to all. They believe in you. They invite you to believe in yourself. Your true nature knows the answer. In fact, your real nature *is* the answer. So step forward with the wish to change yourself in a way that transforms and brightens everything else. This new way exists. It exists for you. Accept the invitation.

                                             Vernon Howard

ONE-HUNDRED GUIDES TO VICTORIOUS DAYS

To use these guides, read down the pages and select a topic of special interest to you, perhaps self-command or true security. Next, turn to the page and story indicated. Read the story, letting it tell you all about the topic. Reflect upon the practical power of what you have read, then let the teaching live itself out in daily affairs, naturally and easily.

These guides are excellent for classes and group meetings. The group-leader can select a topic, read the story, and direct the group in a profitable discussion.

1. For absolute proof that you can be happy in the here and now: see page 55—THE HAPPY FUTURE.

2. If you want total and lasting relief from feeling burdened: see page 135—EXHAUSTED DONALD.

3. When you cannot find solutions to the problems of life: see page 84—THE HIGHER ANSWER.

4. How the collapse of your hopes and dreams can turn into a wonderful opportunity: see page 150—INFORMATION FOR BETTY.

5. To realize that self-healing is freely available to all who truly want it: see page 123—TRADER TRAVIS.

6. Why every human being should carefully examine and question his present life: see page 154—THE CHAINS.

7. How to be totally free from feeling oppressed by people and circumstances: see page 105—THE SUPREME LAW.

8. If you want to be a self-commander who does not apologize to anyone: see page 148—THE APOLOGETIC MAN.

9. To read about several people who successfully climbed the cosmic mountain: see page 26—AIDS FOR BEGINNERS.

10. For good news about your search for a higher life: see page 177—PHILIP AND BERNARD.

11. To learn about a gigantic hoax which you must expose: see page 157—THE INNOCENT JEWELER.

12. How to see life in an astonishingly new way: see page 31—HOW TO LISTEN.

13. If you do not know what to do about feelings of insecurity: see page 161—AT THE KING'S COMMAND.

14. When you want to feel right about yourself and everything else: see page 136—THE RIGHT FEELING.

15. How to remain in a happy independence from all kinds of exterior happenings: see page 91—RISING AND FALLING FORTUNES.

16. Why you should never attribute power to fear and anxiety: see page 107—TUNNELS.

17. If you do not want to feel depressed or to be made nervous by external events: see page 140—PAUL AND LEWIS.

18. For a spiritual law which can work for you in your human relations: see page 46—THE OPENING IN THE WALL.

19. If you want several helpful truths to reflect upon today: see page 194—SOMETHING TRUE.

20. When you do not know what to do about frantically rushing thoughts: see page 71—THE INTERVAL.

21. If you want to stop unhappy events before they reach you: see page 176—SIGNS OF A STORM.

22. How to be totally free from painful decisions regarding other people: see page 47—NO NEED TO THINK.

23. To profit from a group of men and women who have found real riches: see page 102—HELPFUL STATEMENTS.

24. To permit your mind to give you accurate guidance every day: see page 72—THE REVOLVING WHEEL.

25. How to become a psychic magician who can make ob-

stacles disappear forever: see page 114—THE STRANGE MAGICIANS.

26. When you feel a need to go on to greater discoveries: see page 185—OPAL COUNTRY.

27. To read about several right actions by which you can live your own life: see page 31—RIGHT ACTION.

28. If you ever feel all alone while on your cosmic course: see page 58—AT THE BROOK.

29. How to advance yourself by seeing things as they really are: see page 70—AT THE PALACE.

30. For an interesting adventure which increases consciousness and insight: see page 125—THE GREAT DIFFERENCE.

31. Why you should make inner and individual transformation the foremost business of your life: see page 97—THE POWER OF REFUSAL.

32. When you want to listen to guidance which is always right: see page 166—THE SIX WITNESSES.

33. How an understanding of fear and worry ends their tyranny: see page 117—HOWLING WOLVES.

34. Why you should determine to become a bit more conscious every day: see page 68—BOXES OF SILVER.

35. For a clear summary of an important fact about your life: see page 160—HIGHER CONSCIOUSNESS.

36. To hear helpful answers given to one perplexed man: see page 190—SEEKER AND TEACHER.

37. If you ever feel overwhelmed by a flood of difficulties: see page 87—HOW TO MAKE EVERYTHING DIFFERENT.

38. When you do not know whether someone is giving you accurate guidance or not: see page 98—THE TRUE AND THE FALSE.

39. If you wish to increase your speed along the cosmic path: see page 20—A MISTAKE TO AVOID.

40. For information which will restore freshness to anyone's life: see page 181—THE FLOURISHING TREE.

41. To understand the fundamental cause of man's heartache and confusion: see page 56—ILLUSION.

42. For freedom from negative emotions which block happiness: see page 133–THE ROCK.

43. Why one man gave up his self-defeating ways to attend classes in esotericism: see page 38–GILBERT'S STORY.

44. If you want to collect some practical facts about people and their ways: see page 48–REVELATIONS ABOUT HUMAN NATURE.

45. For keys which unlock the secret of individual liberty and independence: see page 152–CLASS IN WISCONSIN.

46. If you wish to swiftly collect the answers to life: see page 130–IN THE BAKERY.

47. To free the mind from a wrong reaction which causes panic: see page 115–THE CREEPER.

48. To learn about a spiritual law that changes and uplifts your exterior conditions: see page 83–HOW TO MAKE LIFE EASIER.

49. For vital facts about healing and refreshment: see page 23–THE SECRET STREAM.

50. When you want to see how other people have succeeded in the cosmic adventure: see page 142–THE OPEN SEA.

51. When you wish to attract authentic needs: see page 34 –THE SIGNAL-DRUMS.

52. For news about a rich inheritance which is waiting for you: see page 27–THE KING'S VOICE.

53. To read about a great secret for self-healing: see page 139–HOW TO USE SORROW.

54. If you want to know of one rich reward which comes to the self-awakened person: see page 130–WHAT AN AWAKENED MAN SEES.

55. When you are unable to understand why your life has so many pains and sorrows: see page 167–HOW PAIN VANISHES.

56. To learn how one class member used these principles to enter a new world: see page 121–ACTRESS ANN.

57. How you can make your life unfold in a different and happier way: see page 180–WHAT HAPPENED TO EVELYN.

58. How to see the world and everyone in it with perfect clarity and understanding: see page 74–THE MAYOR.

59. To hear some cheery statements from men and women who are succeeding: see page 62–ENCOURAGEMENT.

60. If you want one fact which can end a thousand tensions and pressures: see page 112–UNEXPECTED EVENTS.

61. How to awaken to a new and true confidence that remains always: see page 25–THE EGYPTIAN SOLDIER.

62. When you do not know what to do about the problem of loneliness: see page 86–THE COUNTRY WOMAN.

63. To discover how one woman conquered guilt and resentment and found true goodness: see page 45–THE TRULY GOOD WOMAN.

64. If you are ever anxious over the future and its changes: see page 178–HOW TO HANDLE CHANGE.

65. To read about a marvelous and victorious way of thinking: see page 75–THE THIRD WAY OF THINKING.

66. For an example of the great practical benefit of these higher truths: see page 104–GLENN'S STORY.

67. To see how self-investigation can solve the mysteries in your life: see page 169–THE STRANGE ROAD.

68. How one student discovered an extraordinary secret about daily life: see page 66–HOW TO USE LIFE.

69. To have a life which is abundant with everything you really want: see page 195–THE ALERT SENTRY.

70. To read how several men and women corrected their self-defeating behavior: see page 111–CORRECTED MISTAKES.

71. If you want to command both yourself and your daily affairs: see page 16–THE DREAMER.

72. For an explanation which can change and uplift your entire life: see page 187–THE STATE OF AWARENESS.

73. When you wish a reminder of why human beings behave as they do: see page 42–MECHANICAL MAN.

74. Why one man made esoteric teachings his great passion in life: see page 148–WHAT CLAUDE SAW.

75. To discover the secret of one man's dynamic and profitable action: see page 29–THE MAN WHO READ HIMSELF.

76. To learn what it really means to be a free and independent individual: see page 126—WHAT A FREE MAN IS LIKE.

77. If you want to be your own accurate guide through life: see page 39—IN THE FOG.

78. How to understand what love is really all about: see page 143—THE NATURE OF TRUE LOVE.

79. When you wish to increase the power and efficiency of your mind: see page 73—RIGHT THINKING.

80. If you want to enter the free and natural flow of life: see page 96—LET LIFE FLOW.

81. When you want powers which have worked for others and which can also work for you: see page 164—SELF-ADVANCING STATEMENTS.

82. For an important lesson which should be kept in mind at all times: see page 109—A REAL SOURCE OF HELP.

83. Why you should start today to become your own psychological atmosphere: see page 173—GEORGE AND LUCY.

84. If you want to find the one authority who can provide every answer you need: see page 191—SLIPS OF PAPER.

85. To discover in just a few seconds how you can be forever free from all disappointment: see page 63—THE TWO BALLOONS.

86. If you do not like the taste of your present life: see page 160—THE NEW FRUIT.

87. If you want to enter an entirely new world of wonder and nobility: see page 52—THE TAPESTRY.

88. To read about several students who banished painful confusion from their lives: see page 137—THE END OF CONFUSION.

89. If you want to use your very feelings of emptiness to find genuine satisfaction: see page 153—THE SELF-COMMANDING KING.

90. Why the man who finds himself no longer drives himself into exhaustion see page 128—RICH AND FAMOUS.

91. When other people do not understand why you give your time and energy to inner exploration: see page 50—THE DRIVER.

92. To discover the wonderful way to never again feel mistreated by other people: see page 82—INWARD INVESTIGATION.

93. How you can enjoy life under all conditions: see page 179—RAIN.

94. When you no longer know which way to turn to solve a problem: see page 22—HIGHER HELP.

95. How you can become the supreme commander of everything in life: see page 85—THE SECRET OF THE AGES.

96. Why you should never listen to advice from those who do not want the truth: see page 192—WHAT THE LECTURER SAW.

97. For vital information which can end personal suffering: see page 60—SUFFERING MUST BE STUDIED.

98. Why you should remove many opinions and theories from your mind: see page 95—SECRET CODES.

99. To remind yourself of what you should seek from your study of this book: see page 32—QUESTION IN BOSTON.

100. If you want to know the sure way to live in a higher world: see page 78—THE KIND OF WORLD.

Chapter 1

YOU CAN NOW ENTER A WORLD OF WONDER

THE DREAMER

There was once a man who loved to dream. In his dreams he saw himself as a great and powerful person who was adored by everyone. He dreamed so often that he began to believe that his dreams were realities, and so also thought that realities were dreams. So in his relations with the world his dreams were in command.

Misery. Other people did not treat him according to his dreams. Worse, to his fiery indignation, others had their own dreams in which they expected *him* to honor *them*.

Studying his pain, he traced it back to his insistence upon living out his dreams. That began his awakening. The day came when the man lived from himself, not from his dreams, which gave him command of both himself and his daily affairs.

Our first and last task is to understand the meaning of self-awakening and then awaken to our true nature.

MENTAL PROGRESS

There was once an earnest man who had succeeded in

the spiritual journey. He had traveled all the way from desert to mountaintop. Someone asked him how his thinking had changed along the way. Taking pen and paper, the successful man revealed his step by step mental progress:

"I know."

"I may not know."

"I do not know."

"I would like to know."

"I will try to know."

"I know."

True spiritual knowledge is acquired through an honest admission of a lack of knowledge.

THE ENCHANTING BELL

A temple on a hilltop possessed a bell with enchanting tones. The citizens of a village some distance away could hear the tones only faintly and occasionally. Wanting to hear the bell clearly and more often, the citizens made their request to the man in charge of the temple.

"To hear the bell as you wish," replied the man, "you must enter the temple and ring the bell for yourself. You are invited to do so."

Those who accepted the invitation heard the enchanting bell whenever they wanted it.

The ring of truth will be heard by all who accept personally the invitation to hear it.

HOW TO USE WEARINESS

A newcomer to a study group in New Jersey remarked to the teacher, "I am curious about a point made last week. You said we have to be utterly weary in order to qualify for a new life. What does this mean?"

Said the teacher to the rest of the class, "Please answer the gentleman's question. What weariness brought you here?"

Herbert responded, "I was thoroughly exhausted by my nervous pretense that all was well with me."

Said Vera, "Weariness with popular answers that answered nothing brought me here."

Jack replied, "I was tired of trying to please people who demanded more every time you pleased them."

Laura said, "It was too fatiguing to stumble through every day without knowing what my life was all about."

Awareness of personal confusion is the first intelligent act of anyone who no longer wants to live that way.

THE TRUTH IS WITHIN

A man and his young son lived in a country torn with conflict and foolishness. The father wished above all for his son to grow up into a sane and decent human being. Since the people of the land called evil good and called good evil, the father acted intelligently. He sewed a book of true wisdom into the lining of his son's coat.

Years later, following his father's example of goodness, the son sought the true answers to life. His diligent search soon enabled him to distinguish between society's appearances of truth and actual truth. Then one day he found the book of wisdom placed inside the coat so many years earlier. The son knew the book told the truth, for something within him matched that truth.

Every bit of true knowledge you read in a book can be experienced directly and personally within, for knowledge is never apart from your awakened nature.

THE THREE LEARNERS

About to take a journey, a teacher decided to take one of his disciples as an assistant. Calling three learners before him, he said, "On this trip you will meet many upsetting experiences. How will you handle them for inner profit?"

Said one disciple, "I will imitate your responses to them."

The second man answered, "I will fight them and hope to win."

Said the third disciple, "I will calmly study my own reactions to them."

The third disciple was chosen.

Freedom from upsetting experiences begins with impartial self-observation, for that creates self-understanding.

THE UNHEALTHY ATMOSPHERE

A secret factory in a forgotten desert constantly poured an invisible and unhealthy gas into the atmosphere. The gas reached the unsuspecting people in distant cities, making their lives a melancholy muddle.

Wondering what was wrong, a scientist made a quiet and independent investigation. He finally traced the trouble back to the secret factory. He tried to tell others about it, but they dismissed him as a strange alarmist. The people believed the air was not only quite normal, but the only kind of air possible.

But the scientist saved himself by learning to breathe in a special way. Though living within the poisonous atmosphere, he was immune to it.

There are some people who cannot accept human sickness as normal and necessary, and your task is to become one of them.

THE STRANGER WITH THE WHEAT

A country had such severe weather all year long that its farmers could produce only inferior crops of wheat. One day a stranger rode into the farmlands with a sack of wheat seeds. However, the stranger spoke a strange language which the farmers could not understand. Knowing this, the stranger used gestures and physical objects in an attempt to convey a message about his wheat. But the distrustful farmers and their wives made little effort to understand.

Aware of their suspicion and lack of receptivity, the stranger rode away. He took with him the new and sturdy wheat seeds which produced abundant harvests in all kinds of weather.

Because men neither understand nor try to understand the language of higher truth, they fail to reap richer harvests.

A MISTAKE TO AVOID

Clifford requested, "To help us avoid mistakes along the path, what is a common mistake made by beginners?"

"People do not see the enormous difference between mere self-improvement and a deep change of inner nature. The great difference is this. Self-improvement, such as learning better grammar or a foreign language, never challenges a man's false ideas about himself. But inner transformation requires him to hear facts about himself that he does not want to hear. Only a teaching which makes a man face himself as he is, with all his hidden confusions, can develop a truly new kind of person."

Wholeness exists when the inner and the outer are the same, and this is attained by seeing the inner as it actually is, not as it is imagined.

THE SMALL BOX

A poor man asked a wealthy friend for lessons in becoming a successful merchant. Consenting, the rich man also gave a small box to his friend. Looking inside, the puzzled poor man saw nothing, but gratefully took it home.

After many lessons, the rich man said, "Concealed in the box is a gold coin for you. Invest it and you will be successful."

Asked the poor man, "Why did you not tell me of it before?"

"Because you would not have known how to use it. You might have spent it foolishly, or used it to impress friends. But thanks to your faithful attention to lessons, you are now a wise investor."

Opportunitities for spiritual success appear just as swiftly as we make ourselves ready for them.

THE BARREL OF WATER

A man who lived in the desert brought a barrel of pure water to his cabin.

The first day he added some sugar to make it taste sweeter.

On the second day he mixed in some coloring to give it a bright appearance.

The next day he made it thicker by adding some syrup.

On the fourth day he tossed in some ginger to give it a spicy taste.

Every day he drank from the barrel which no longer contained pure water. And there were two strange things about it. He could never figure out why the water never tasted right. And he could never remember that he himself was responsible for the contents of the barrel.

Man distorts the pure truth, never seeing his own involvement and never realizing the ruinous consequences.

THE RARE SPICE

The hobby of a woman in Kansas was the growing of rare spices. One day she received a sample of a spice completely new to her. It so excited her taste she was eager to grow it for herself. Not knowing its source, she made inquiries, but without results. Unable to forget the taste of the rare spice, she put more energy into her search. Dozens of letters were mailed. Notices were inserted in magazines for gardeners.

After a long and disappointing search, a letter arrived from Argentina. "I know what you want," the writer stated, "and I can help you." The needed information followed.

"Thank heaven," breathed the woman. "There is someone who knows!"

Those who know the truth are available to whoever cannot forget his first taste of something totally new.

HIGHER HELP

In the early days of aviation a pilot was forced down in a remote region of Brazil. Hiking to a distant village, he asked for help from the natives. Though not understanding what it was all about, the natives helped the pilot place tree branches in an open field, arranged in a definite manner.

When a rescuing airplane appeared overhead, the pilot explained that the branches spelled out *HELP*. The natives then understood how rescue could come from a higher source previously unknown to them.

There is something in you which is far wiser than anything in the world of men.

ALAN'S QUESTION

"May we have," said Alan, "an example of how we unknowingly stand in our own way?"

"No barrier is thicker than to pretend to understand something which is far from understood. Take someone who advises a lonely friend to get involved in social activities. But the advisor himself is secretly lonely, even while having his own social escapes. Never having honestly examined himself, he is unaware of pretending to understand what is not understood. Incidentally, loneliness is simply a result of living apart from the Whole."

A common barrier to self-understanding is the careless assumption that one already understands himself.

MOUNT BLISS

A man who was neither healthy nor happy heard about an invigorating herb which grew on top of a place called Mount Bliss. Not sure of its location, he studied a map and went on his way. While climbing upward he met a mountaineer who discouraged him from continuing.

"But a powerful herb grows on top of Mount Bliss."

"True."

"And it supplies fresh health and strength."

"Correct."

"Then why should I stop climbing?"

"Because you are not climbing Mount Bliss."

When seeking self-restoration we must make sure we are climbing in the right place, which these ideas help to do.

THE BAFFLED STUDENT

A sincere but baffled student told his teacher, "I want to wake up, but the lessons sometimes cause distress. Is it necessary to mention our faulty ways so often?"

Replied the teacher, "Do you remember what happened yesterday? You were walking next to a dangerous cliff you could not see because of the bushes. What was my motive in telling you about your position?"

The student never again brought up the subject.

At first we think the truth shouts out in harsh condemnation, but later we see it as a gentle invitation.

THE SECRET STREAM

A woman heard of a secret stream flowing with healing waters. Taking the single path to the stream, she dipped her jar into it. She found that the water was indeed pure and healthful. Hearing about it, the woman's friends hastened to the secret stream, each carrying his own jar filled with the kind of water they drank habitually. "We had better compare this stream with our own water," they advised each other.

But the secret stream had a unique feature. To produce health, the water had to be placed into the empty jar of each person. Many people were unwilling to empty their jars of the old water, and so denied themselves a healing. But the wise ones threw out the old contents of the jars and received the desired healing.

By higher law, the new will be given as soon as the old is given up.

SUNNY SLOPES

Philip told this story to other members of the study group: "As a boy I once walked among some snowy hills with my father and some neighboring farmers. They wanted to know which slopes were capable of growing new crops. It was easy to determine. While snow fell on all the slopes, some were in a position to catch the sunshine which melted the snow. The slopes on the shady side could grow nothing."

Philip concluded, "Likewise, we must expose ourselves to the sunshine of cosmic facts. When yesterday's mental snows are melted, a harvest is certain."

Place yourself in a receptive position to healing powers.

VIEW AND VIEWER

A husband and wife managed a tourist lodge in the mountains. One day a tourist arrived who displayed an irritable nature from the very start. He complained about the food, the service, and much more.

Early one morning the manager invited the guests out to the balcony. He explained that weather conditions were perfect for viewing a beautiful sunrise. Accepting, the guests stood there and saw a colorful scene of dawn in the mountains.

The irritable man left the balcony and marched sourly past the manager's wife. Wondering about it, she later asked her husband, "Something wrong with the view?"

"Something wrong with the viewer."

A man's own mind makes his world whatever it is, for view and viewer are the same.

DIFFERENT FOOD

A sick man consulted a specialist who told him, "You need a different kind of food. Dine somewhere else."

Before the specialist could say more, the man rushed out to begin dining at different cafes. But, remaining sick, he returned to the specialist, who said, "Excellent! Now you know what *won't* work. Go to this place," said the specialist, offering an address.

Arriving there, the man was greeted by a woman holding a book. "Ah," she welcomed him, "I see you have been to the specialist. Here is your different food."

She handed him a volume of higher truth.

The different diet of esoteric knowledge restores and maintains spiritual health.

THE EGYPTIAN SOLDIER

An Egyptian soldier of ancient days faithfully served the army physicians as an assistant. Feeling ill himself one evening, he tried to contact the doctors. A captain told him, "After a long day on the battlefield, all the doctors are asleep." The soldier persisted, but the captain only repeated that the physicians were sleeping.

"But have you heard the good news?" said the captain with a sudden smile. "By Pharoah's decree you are now a physician yourself!"

Gaining new self-confidence at the news, the soldier diagnosed and healed his own illness.

The healing facts coming through a teacher are the same healing facts already existing within you, so your task is to awaken these slumbering physicians.

WHY PRETENSE MUST GO

A man was very proud of his health and energy. But one day he fell ill, so his wife called a doctor. The man resisted the doctor while angrily denying his illness. In a private talk, the doctor explained to the wife, "The whole problem is your husband's precious self-image of being a healthy man. It stands in the way of recovery."

"But what can we do?" asked the wife.

"As long as he deceives himself, nothing can be done. Suffering must shatter his pretense. If you see signs of this, call me, for I have just the medicine he needs."

The only way to recover from spiritual illness is to abandon deceptive self-images and acknowledge the illness.

AIDS FOR BEGINNERS

Some advanced students in South Carolina offered these aids for beginners on the path:

Dennis: "To get to the point in life you must know what the point is, and the point is to wake up."

Edna: "Your single greatest mistake will be a refusal to listen to truth for fear it will rob you of something valuable. But truth wants only to take your distress."

William: "The seeker becomes the finder when he does not seek merely what he *wants* to find."

Ruby: "People want exciting things to happen to them. If you want a happening that changes your world, continue to learn."

Kenneth: "See how many distractions you can ignore while climbing the mountain."

Stick to the point of cosmic self-awakening.

THE BUILDERS

There was once a barren land where wood was scarce. But a certain citizen knew of a hidden forest where wood was plentiful, so he availed himself of it. When people asked for some of his timber he asked, "What will you do with it?"

Those who wanted firewood were politely turned away. But citizens who wished to build homes or cabinets or boxes were given the wood they needed.

Truth is for those who wish to use it constructively.

THE KING'S VOICE

The young son of a king was kidnapped by evil men and carried away to a distant land. The prince grew to manhood, not knowing of his royal inheritance.

Over the years the king had kept a request before his ambassadors in foreign lands: "Look for young men who resemble my son, and send them to the palace." When a young man arrived a test was arranged to see whether the king's voice was recognized. The king and several of his advisors stood behind a screen. Each spoke a few words to the young man on the other side.

One day the prince himself stood there and dimly recognized his father's voice. Further investigation proved that he was indeed the rightful heir to the throne.

No matter how long we have been absent, the voice of truth can be recognized by those who listen energetically.

A PRACTICAL SUMMARY OF CHAPTER 1

1. Seek to understand the meaning of self-awakening, for that is the greatest task on earth.

2. The person who listens persistently for the ring of truth will find it within himself.

3. It is truly intelligent to simply admit that one does not know, for that leads to knowing.

4. Build self-acquaintance by observing your thoughts and actions, which results in self-liberty.

5. Never accept unhappiness and confusion as normal and necessary, for they can be ended completely.

6. While the truth may seem shocking at first, it turns out to be the kindest friend you could want.

7. A willingness to abandon the old and the useless makes room for the new and the beneficial.

8. Think of receptivity to truth as a great power for self-elevation, for it is just that.

9. Make it the point of your life to discover this totally new kind of life.

10. Regardless of how far or how long an individual has wandered, the truth rejects no one, but accepts everyone.

Chapter 2

KEYS TO ACTION OF ABUNDANT PROFIT

THE MAN WHO READ HIMSELF

A man once owned a book he prized highly, entitled, *How to Behave in Life*. When not knowing what to do he consulted the book. However, there was a major difficulty. He could read the book only when in a lighted place, and he often found himself in dark and strange situations. So when unable to read the book he often stumbled or bluffed his way through perplexing situations.

Wishing something better, he determined to be his own book. So with earnest self-study he understood both himself and surrounding life. Reading both of them accurately, he behaved *from himself*. And wherever he went he never again stumbled or bluffed, but behaved perfectly.

The person who understands what he himself is all about will also comprehend what life is all about.

ESOTERIC EDUCATION

Inquired Edward, a new student in class, "What is the difference between an esoteric education and ordinary schooling?"

"Suppose you study to be a doctor. What are you doing? Filling *memory* with facts and experiences. So memory-education makes you a doctor, but not a whole man, for the doctor could get depressed. In esoteric education the *whole man* is enlightened and harmonized. A complete man is never depressed because *his* memory never insists he must be the most popular doctor in town. A fragmented man compares himself with others, which is not the way of a man with an esoteric education."

Intellectual knowledge has its place in everyday affairs, but only total insight can lift us above everyday life.

THE SPIRITUAL EXERCISE

A pupil asked his teacher, "Please give me a spiritual exercise."

Instructed the teacher, "Sweep the floor."

"But I'd like to have a spiritual exercise."

"Sweep the floor while being aware of your sweeping."

"But I always do it that way."

"No, you sweep mechanically, with your mind a mile away. Anything performed consciously is a spiritual exercise."

The next day the student asked, "May I have another spiritual exercise?"

"Wash the dishes."

True spirituality consists of doing whatever we do with a conscious mind, a mind which remains where the action is.

THE MUSICIAN

There was once a land where music was unknown. One day a wandering musician came to town and played his flute in public. The citizens were enthralled by the lilting tunes. Crowding around the musician they pleaded, "Show us how to make music!"

The musician handed the people a spare flute. Several of them blew into it, but when no music came out, they looked bewildered and disappointed. "There is something wrong with this flute," complained several people.

"It takes patient practice to make music," explained the musician. "Listen, and I will show you how to do it."

When hearing that they had to do certain things to make music, many of the people lost interest and walked away.

Spiritual music can be played by those who do the right and the necessary things.

RIGHT ACTION

A lecture in esotericism was delivered in Vancouver, Canada, on the topic of right action. In summary, the lecturer said, "For right action, use every experience for additional insight. Consistently challenge your present ways of thinking. Realize that your thoughts create your psychological surroundings. Through awareness and wisdom, do not permit other people to become a problem to you. Do not run away from unpleasant facts about yourself. Never attempt to gain power or authority over anyone. React to daily events with clear thought, not with mechanical emotions. Learn to recognize self-defeating behavior and refuse it. Patiently absorb one lesson at a time."

The lecture concluded, "Live your own life with right action."

Right action is anything which adds to self-awareness.

HOW TO LISTEN

A teacher asked a group of new pupils, "Did it ever occur to you that there might be an entirely new way to see life than your present way? I will show you this astonishing way, but first you must learn to listen. For the next fifteen minutes please study what I have written on the blackboard." The students read:

Listen with present opinions set aside.
Listen with an eagerness to learn.
Listen with no desire to dispute.

Listen without ego-protection.
Listen with a wish to become new.
Listen with wonder at this marvelous way.
    To hear the answers—which certainly exist—we must
first recognize and dissolve our own resistances to them.

TURNIPS

Two foolish men lived next door to each other. Both were
so gullible they believed anything anyone told them. One
day one of them wanted to grow turnips in his back yard,
but did not want to spend money for turnip seeds.

"You don't need real seeds," his neighbor told him.
"Write *turnip seed* on several bits of paper and plant
them. That is what I was told."

The other man did as he was told. A week later he asked
his advisor, "Do you really believe turnips can grow from
those bits of paper?"

"Well," drawled his neighbor, "I did hear of one man
who ended up with paper turnips."

Artificial actions bring artificial results.

AT THE OASIS

An Arabian salt merchant reached an oasis, where he
requested water for the rest of his journey. When a man
asked, "Where is your jar?" the merchant admitted he had
lost it.

The man gestured to another part of the oasis. "There is
plenty of clay over there. I can give you water, but you
must make your own jar."

Through diligent self-study we can prepare ourselves
to receive the inspirations we need.

QUESTION IN BOSTON

In a class in Boston the teacher asked his students,
"What do you want from your studies?" These replies were
selected as the best:

"I want to be comfortable with myself, not through power or possessions, but because life is understood at last."

"It is my wish to end the tension of trying to prove myself right by actually being right within."

"I wish to reach the level where I am not offended by the truth, but healed by it."

"Since I sense how artificiality causes anxiety, that is reason enough for me to abolish artificiality."

"I want to live undeceived by myself and by everyone else."

"Through these principles I wish to halt problems and troublesome involvements before they happen."

You will always go right by preferring mental enlightenment to emotional arousal.

THE VALUE OF ATTENTION

An experienced forest guide was hired by some people who wanted to explore the woods. He knew it was first necessary to destroy their false confidence in themselves. Pointing to a hilltop beyond the woods he directed, "Fix your attention on that hill and climb it in a minimum of time."

When the puffing hikers reached the hilltop they found the guide waiting for them. "Do you know why you are so late?" he asked. "You were distracted by the sights along the way. Had you kept your attention on this hilltop you would not have lost your way."

Do not be distracted by superficial attractions, but keep your attention on the spiritual hilltop you want to reach.

THE BASKET

Standing over a table, a teacher held a small basket in one hand and several grapes in the other hand. One by one he dropped the grapes into the basket, but all fell through to land on the table.

Said the teacher, "You will now remember that unhealthy desires and illusory ambitions always fall into a bottomless basket. They can neither accumulate nor satisfy. End wasteful actions by understanding this."

True advancement begins with the realization that everything we have done up to now has not really advanced us one inch.

THE SIGNAL-DRUMS

Many years ago an explorer in Africa set out along the Zambezi River, with Victoria Falls as his final destination. As he pushed forward he devised a system of signals to summon supplies to him at any point in the journey. Natives with signal-drums were placed in a line along the trail, each man within hearing distance of the next man. When supplies were needed, the drums sent out a message across jungles and hills.

But when the explorer reached Victoria Falls, something went wrong with the signals. The reason was discovered. Some of the drummers had wandered away from their posts, while others had handled the messages carelessly. When they were replaced with reliable men, the signals brought the needed supplies promptly.

Vigilant thoughts and feelings supply our every need.

THE RIGHT START

"We wish a right start in these classes," said Lee, a member of a new study group. "May we have some direction?"

"Start as if you know nothing at all about the way out. Now of course this is insulting to vanity and frightening to hardened thought. Do it anyway. Vanity and hardened thought can only keep you in dismal prison. Dare to not know the answers, dare to discard silly superstition which masquerades as respectable tradition. Do this ten times a day, every time you feel tempted to pretend you know what you are talking about. Pretense is the very prison itself. Begin every day with the wonderment of not knowing what life is all about. This is true power, refreshment and relief. Eventually, a new feeling of rightness will arise within."

You can make a new right start every single second, for your real nature is not chained by five minutes or fifty years ago.

THE TREACHEROUS ROCKS

A wandering tribe settled along the bank of a rushing river. The land on the other side of the river looked pleasant, so the people placed large rocks in the water in an attempt to walk across. But the stones shifted positions so treacherously that the people splashed down into the water, cold and irritable. Their failure continued over the years.

Oddly, whenever a stranger wanted to reach the other shore, the villagers recommended the rocks. More oddly, few strangers ever asked, "How come you recommend the rocks when they have done nothing but make you miserable and frustrated?"

No matter how traditional or how highly recommended, false methods for reaching the other shore can only cause frustration.

WHAT FEW MEN SEE

A seeker wished to enroll in the school of a wise man. The teacher instructed, "Go out and be good."

The seeker went out and walked down the streets, giving gifts to the poor and helping whoever needed help.

When returning to the wise man he was told, "I asked you to *be* good, not *do* good. There is a great difference, which few men see. You *did* good without *being* good, for you had a motive of self-reward."

When the seeker nodded the teacher said, "You were already in school but did not know it. Think about your first lesson."

Above visible good works is a higher goodness which flows effortlessly and without thought.

THE INCOMPETENT DOG

A shepherd owned a dog which was unable to understand its duties in handling sheep. The shepherd placed his dog in the company of other dogs who performed their tasks expertly. The shepherd hoped his dog would observe the others and learn from them.

But the dog remained as incompetent as before, so the shepherd asked a friend for advice. The friend said, "Merely being in good company changes nothing. You must show your dog the advantages of right action."

Association with higher truth can change only those who feel the need for self-transformation.

ACCEPT THE ACTIONS

Asked a student at a class in New York, "How can we get more from these lectures?"

"Accept the actions as well as the words. If I tell you it is wise to learn something from every experience you will agree wholeheartedly. But do you *do* it? You may agree that sunshine is healthy, but it does no good if you remain indoors."

"That is true, but how can we distinguish between artificial action and movements having real meaning?"

"The only test of action is whether it *truly* changes the kind of human being you are. All else is illusion masquerading as reality."

Never hesitate to perform authentic action, for results can never be anything but good.

CUP AND CABBAGE

A teacher realized that the girls in her cooking class had picked up several wrong methods. Knowing they had some unlearning to do, the teacher provided a visual lesson. She placed a cup and a cabbage on a table, then instructed one of the girls, "Hold one hand in back of you and pick up the cabbage."

When the girl had done so, the teacher said, "Now pick up the cup."

"I can't," said the girl.

"Why not?"

"My hand is filled with the cabbage."

"Then drop the cabbage."

By dropping wrong and impractical methods we are free to grasp right procedures.

AT THE DOORWAY

Dinner was about to be served at a school of higher truth. A teacher wished to impart a special lesson, so he told his students, "Stand at the doorway of the dining room and talk about food for ten minutes."

When the students finished the teacher said, "Explain the lesson."

Someone volunteered, "Mere talk about truth leaves one empty."

Idle talking and mechanical thinking about right ideas is not the same as living from those ideas, so we must advance to the living.

SAND CASTLES

Two boys began to build sand castles on the seashore. One of them chose a site several yards above the topmost reach of the waves. The other boy built his castle close to the waves which battered his walls and towers. Through the constant need to make repairs, the boy learned to build a strong castle which waves could not damage.

The castle of the other boy had no contact with the waves, so he never learned how to make it sturdy. When an unusually high wave smashed against his castle, it melted.

A sturdy interior castle arises not by retreating from the pounding waves of life, but by meeting them with cosmic consciousness.

GILBERT'S STORY

During a class session, Gilbert told how he had been attracted to esoteric teachings:

"For many years I felt like a man who endlessly crosses an old bridge which is about to collapse. I don't know whether any of you have ever crossed a dangerous bridge, but as a boy in Kentucky I had to use one every morning. I felt uneasy when approaching it and nervous when crossing. I sensed there was something wrong with what was under my feet."

Gilbert continued, "The same feeling drew me to this class. I sensed something wrong with my life. I could no longer accept my own flattering evaluation of myself. So here I am, and it's about time."

There is another way to live, which unfolds before those who earnestly and persistently question their present ways.

A SECRET FOR STEADY SUCCESS

An enthusiastic mountaineer climbed to the peak of what was believed to be the highest mountain in the land. He rested in satisfaction until hearing of the existence of an even higher peak, which he then climbed and conquered. His pride in himself lasted only until told about a third mountain which towered above the other two. He scaled to its top at once.

By this time the mountaineer had learned something, so he philosophized, "Never again will I assume I have reached the highest peak."

The secret of steady success is to detect and abolish self-defeating assumptions.

EXAMINE AND CORRECT

"What would you do," a teacher asked his students, "if your automobile broke down?"

"Examine and correct," said someone.

"What if your television set became faulty?"

"Examine and correct."

"What do people do when their lives become faulty?"

Smiling, the students remained silent. Said the teacher, "You smile because you know people can be quite practical with cars and television but show not an ounce of sense toward their damaged lives. Tell them to examine and correct and it sounds too simple. They want mysterious formulas and exciting entertainments. There is more health in eating one cherry than in reading a whole book about cherries."

Remember that what society calls creative action may be called foolish tragedy by Reality.

THE CELESTIAL CITY

An unhappy man heard of a place called Celestial City, where everyone lived in bliss. Gathering all his belongings into several packages, he traveled until reaching the City's narrow gate. He tried to enter, but his large packages prevented him from succeeding.

"To enter Celestial City," said a voice on the inside, "you must drop everything you now consider valuable."

To penetrate the new we must first abandon habitual attitudes and preferences.

IN THE FOG

Asked a student in class, "What is humanity like?"

Answered the teacher, "Man is like a motorist driving in a thick fog. He anxiously follows the lights of the car ahead, hoping the driver knows where he is going."

"How can we escape such anxiety?"

"There is no fog for you except your own fog. Escape it through inner action and you will never anxiously follow anyone else."

Men live in unconscious imitation of each other, then wonder why they are uncomfortable with themselves!

THE INVITATION

A party of boys and girls left their mountain lodge to hike down to a deep valley. Losing their way, they grew anxious. Seeing they were overdue, the manager sent a guide down, who finally found them. On the upward climb, some of the young people asked the guide nervous questions:

"Where are we?"

"On the right path."

"Where are we now?"

"Higher than before."

Wishing to assure them, the guide invited, "Glance upward from time to time. You will glimpse the lodge."

The right path proves itself by providing glimpses of something higher than ourselves.

REVIEW THESE STEPS TO USEFUL ACTION

1. When living from our true nature we see what life is all about, which delivers self-command.

2. Every day practice the art of doing whatever you do with an alert and conscious mind.

3. Right action consists of anything which contributes to self-knowledge and self-unity.

4. Artificial causes bring artificial results, so a study of originating action is good and necessary.

5. Do not permit shallow attractions to pull your attention away from your cosmic destination.

6. Remember that every new second is a fresh start, for you are never chained by the past of ten seconds or ten years ago.

7. The person who performs spiritual right actions will certainly feel right.

8. A clear awareness of the self-punishment in wrong action gives us the courage to drop it.

9. You can live from cosmic facts, rather than from human assumptions, because your real nature knows the difference in the two.

10. There is something much loftier than habitual thinking, so your pleasant task is to rise to it.

Chapter 3

HOW TO SUCCEED IN HUMAN RELATIONS

MECHANICAL MAN

A class in cosmic consciousness met one Saturday afternoon at the home of a member. The topic of discussion was the unpredictable and savage behavior of human beings. "Man preaches peace," said Audrey, "but delights in war. What is it all about?"

Nodding toward the window, the teacher said, "See that automobile out there? Suppose you preached a sermon to that car in which you instructed it to never run wild and cause a wreck. Would it obey? No, because the car is mechanical, and can behave only on the level of mechanicalness. Likewise, man is mechanical, which is why events happen the way they do. Only a conscious person can behave in a way that does not cause wrecks."

Unconscious negativity is the only cause of human tragedy, and the only cure is consciousness.

THE ARCHER

A teacher and his disciples were crossing a field when they passed an archer who was shooting at a target. When an arrow struck the target in the center the archer praised himself aloud. But when the next arrow missed the target completely the archer angrily blamed a gust of wind.

"Ah," sighed the teacher as the group went on its way. "That is so typical of man. When something goes right it is due to his great skill, but a wrong result is always the fault of someone else."

One goal, which becomes clearer as we progress, is to detect and eliminate self-contradictions.

GIRL FRIENDS

A man had an attractive girl friend with whom he shared many pleasant hours. One day he met another attractive woman, so he said to himself, "I may lose my present girl friend, so to feel secure I will add this second one." But a troubled mind warned, "But by doing this I may lose my present girl." So he agonized in indecision.

He finally decided to add the new sweetheart, and sure enough, he lost the first one. His misery doubled when the new woman turned out to be childish and demanding.

A year later he was again faced with the same problem, but decided to stick with his present girl. Strangely, he still felt insecure. He told himself, "Security must reside on a higher level than my scheming and my decisions. Maybe I can find it."

That was very wise self-informing.

Attempts to find security through decision and choice cannot succeed, for they are products of a divided and therefore unseeing mind.

THE ELOQUENT MONKEY

There was once a monkey who had been trained to read and to speak. As reward and encouragement he was given six peanuts every evening.

One day the monkey was given a book of religion and philosophy, which he memorized. He was then able to deliver impressive lectures on religion and philosophy. Multitudes came for thousands of miles to hear his eloquent messages about love and peace and brotherhood.

One evening the hour came for the monkey to receive his six peanuts. By accident, he was given only five peanuts. Noticing this, the monkey flew into a violent rage. In his fury he tore the book of religion and philosophy into bits.

Hypocrisy is a condition in which a man wrongly believes that mechanical knowledge is the same as a changed nature.

AROUND THE BLOCK

A man had constant dizzy spells for which he could find no cure. He told a friend about it, who advised, "Walk around the block three times on Sunday afternoon."

The man followed the advice, then complained to his friend, "I did what you said, but still feel dizzy."

"It did me no good either."

In trying to understand life, beware of foolish advice from those who do not know.

THE POUNCER

"You have taught us how to listen correctly," said Diane in class, "such as by setting aside hardened opinions. As additional aid, please explain how an insincere person listens to a lecture about truth."

"Like a fox stalking a flock of geese. An enemy of geese, his only aim is to pounce on one of them. It makes no difference which goose he attacks; the attack is all that matters. An insincere listener watches for anything to pounce upon, even the lecturer's way of dressing. This is the listener's desperate attempt to escape the anxiety of hearing truths he does not want to hear. Also, he hopes his pouncing will induce others to do likewise, for he is scared of standing alone. No matter how authoritative or educated he may appear to be, no one is more miserable than a pouncer."

To attack truth in an attempt to escape anxiety over hearing the truth will only increase anxiety.

THE QUIET DOG

A father took his small son on a short business trip to the other side of town. As they approached the client's house, a large dog appeared in the yard, barking furiously. Unable to reach the front door, the father took his son's hand and led him away. The boy looked back at the dog which had become silent. "Why can't we stay?" asked the boy. "The dog is quiet."

"Yes," said the father, "but his barks are still inside."

Never believe that people are what they appear to be.

THE TRULY GOOD WOMAN

A woman who felt guilty over past misdeeds said to herself, "I must repent. I will start by doing good to others."

So she joined charitable organizations and said nice things to people. But to her surprise she felt a vague resentment toward her activities. She felt *forced* to be good. This doubled her guilt, for now she felt guilty over her resentment toward doing good.

Though confused, she intelligently reflected, "There is something dreadfully wrong. This is not goodness at all; it is self-enslaving stage-acting. True goodness must be something entirely different."

So she began a search for true goodness, which she finally found. She explained to herself, "True goodness blooms in the absence of an unconscious self-picture of being good."

Abolish conditioned thoughts about personal goodness and badness and authentic goodness flourishes.

FREEDOM FROM PRETENSE

In order to get what he wanted a man pretended to be a friend of people he secretly scorned. But one day he heard a wise man teach, "Hypocrisy, being self-division, is its own punishment." So with the help of the wise man, the self-divided man became whole and free of pretense.

Later, he met a smooth-talking scoundrel who promised fame and power in return for money. The man declined stating, "No longer my own victim, I am not yours."

A man with no deception in himself cannot be deceived by others.

THE OPENING IN THE WALL

As a clerk in a courtroom, Wayne daily observed human beings in conflict with each other. As part of his inner work, he tried to connect human affairs with the facts absorbed in class, which speeded his progress. At one group gathering he commented, "The best word to describe human relations is *confusion*. Is there some opening in the wall we can work on to make things clearer?"

"You get for yourself exactly what you wish for others—what you *really* wish for others, not what you say you wish. It can be no other way. It is a law of spiritual science. Work with that opening."

Conflict does not enter the life of anyone who understands the spiritual laws governing human relations.

THE WELL-DRESSED AUDIENCE

The people of a certain country did not appreciate truly good music. They preferred noise, which they called music. One day a symphony orchestra visited their country. They did not want its fine music, yet wished to appear cultured and appreciative. So a concert was arranged, which was attended by a large and well-dressed audience.

As the concert progressed, the musicians noticed the bored and inattentive manner of the audience. So one by one the musicians quietly left the stage. The music grew fainter and fainter until it faded out entirely. The half-asleep audience suddenly became aware of the silence. Thinking the concert had ended naturally, the people jumped to their feet and applauded wildly. Then they all went back to the noise which they called music.

The symphonic truth remains only with sincere people who recognize and appreciate it.

NO NEED TO THINK

A teacher provided these answers to an inquirer:

"What if someone wants to leave me?"

"Let him leave."

"What if he wants to stay?"

"Let him stay."

"But what if he is bad for me?"

"If you live from what is true and good, a bad person will not want to stay with you. Your levels have nothing in common. Be true and good yourself, then, you will not even need to think about such things."

Right action is so natural to a true and good person he has no need to think about it.

THE EDUCATED MAN

An educated man who thought he understood human nature asked a stranger, "Would you like to learn about human nature?"

The stranger asked, "May I ask you a question about your own human nature—without offending you?" The question was unexpected, but the educated man nodded, so the stranger asked, "Why do you get secretly angry so often?"

This made the educated man so angry he walked away. He never knew that the stranger really understood human nature. Also, he never knew the stranger could have shown him how to banish hidden anger.

Self-healing alone produces profound knowledge of human nature, and both begin by studying one's own hidden nature.

REVELATIONS ABOUT HUMAN NATURE

Members of a class in Detroit revealed what they had learned about human nature:

James: "Regardless of what they say to the contrary, people always do what they really want to do."

Beatrice: "Whatever makes a man angry has found him out."

Warren: "We rarely see people as they are, but see them according to our own thoughts about them, which must be corrected."

Cecil: "The less a person is able to govern himself the more he is sure he can guide and help others."

Grace: "A man who does not hurt himself cannot be hurt by others."

Neil: "Desire the truth more than you desire friends, for then the friends in your life will be unable to give you trouble."

Insight into human nature as it actually operates is an essential part of your psychic adventure.

THE DICTATOR

There was once a cruel dictator who ruthlessly persecuted everyone who thwarted his ambitions in the smallest way. Having no conscience, he delighted in making everyone as outwardly miserable as he was inwardly tormented.

Finally overthrown by enemies, he fled to another country, where he was forced to live in a small and old house. One day a former enemy was driving by in a car, when the wheels accidentally splashed mud against the house. The tyrant let out a howl of indignation heard a block away.

Remarked an observer, "There is no howl like the howl of a persecutor who feels persecuted."

A man's relationship with others, for peace or discord, will be the same as his relationship with himself.

MAN AND MEDICINE

Feeling ill and weak one day, a man believed he had caught the sickness of some of his neighbors. Slowly making his way to a doctor, the man requested, "Please prescribe some medicine for my neighbors."

"But what about you?" asked the physician.

"No, no, you do not understand," insisted the man as he wearily fell into a chair. "It is my neighbors who are sick."

The man with the illness is the man who needs the medicine.

PERSONAL QUESTIONS

Some newcomers to a truth-lecture were greeted by the teacher's assistant who said, "Since this will be a question and answer session, may I speak frankly with you? Please do not ask personal questions of the teacher. You know, almost everyone wants to know the same things. People are curious as to whether or not he has a sex life. Would you permit people to ask you such a question? People wish to know how long it took him to attain enlightenment. That is asked out of the questioner's anxiety over his own progress. Instead of such wasteful questions, enter into an exploration with the speaker. For instance, ask for guidance in applying the truth to daily affairs, or inquire into the nature of jealousy."

The assistant concluded, "Please keep these points in mind and all of us will have a very profitable session."

Productive results come from listening and reading with productive attitudes.

ON THE SIDEWALK

Two friends met on the sidewalk to hold this conversation:

"How do you feel?"

"Very happy."

"Is everything all right?"

"Just fine."

"Are you really contented?"

"Quite contented."

"Then you had better notify your face."

We can deceive ourselves, but not our actual condition.

ESOTERIC EXPLANATION

"Tell us something about human nature," asked Alex in class.

"The first time you give a man something he falls all over himself in showing his gratitude. The second time he politely thanks you. The third time he is annoyed that you did not bring it sooner. The fourth time he demands twice as much. The fifth time he considers you an enemy to be plundered."

Asked Alex, "What is the esoteric explanation of his behavior?"

"The thrill over the first gifts excites his false sense of self; they seem to affirm him. But the false self is endlessly greedy for thrills, so it suddenly swings over to the new thrill of hatred and violence toward the giver. The false self has no conscience; it has only neurotic desires, which finally wreck the man."

For right human relations, be in social contact with others, but not in wrong psychological involvement with them.

THE DRIVER

Two women were motoring down the highway in a heavy fog. The passenger was one of those unaware people who could never put herself into another person's place. Unable to realize the driver's need to concentrate on the road, the passenger chattered and joked and asked questions. At the end of the hazardous drive the passenger remarked,

"You have been strangely silent for the last hour. You must have had something important on your mind."

"Yes," said the driver. "Your life and mine."

Do not expect other people to understand why your attention is on the road to higher truth.

THE HIGH HILL

Several travelers were lost in the desert. Fortunately, they met a man who was well-acquainted with the region. He instructed, "Climb that high hill over there. The view will show you the way out." One by one the travelers replied:

"My present view is good enough."

"You may be trying to mislead us."

"I already know the way out."

"Have others made it to the hilltop?"

"I am too discouraged to move from here."

"Give us proof of what you say."

"I won't go up there alone."

"With what authority do you advise us?"

Wandering men will do everything but prove the truth by their own investigation.

THE LAW OF ATTRACTION

A tourist who was not noted for deep thinking was traveling through a mountainous region. Wishing to take some photographs of bears, he asked a citizen of a small village where he might find the animals. "Just put out some food," he was advised, "and the bears will come."

An hour later the tourist raced frantically back to the village, frightened and minus his camera. Between gulps of air he gasped, "I put out food for the bears. The bears came."

Whether conscious of it or not, our actions attract the kind of people and conditions in our lives.

INNER CONVERSATIONS

Mr. and Mrs. J. came to say, "We understand the need
to see ourselves as we actually are, not as vanity makes us
think we are. But how can we slip past self-deception to see
what we are really like?"

"You can do it with honest self-observation. Have you
ever noticed the topics of your inner conversations? That is
what you are really like. Observe negative conversations,
such as complaining over betrayal by other people. In positive conversations you quietly talk things over with yourself in an attempt to understand why your life unfolds as it
does. You could then see you were betrayed because of
lack of insight into both your own mind and the minds of
others."

*Return often to the idea that a problem resides in the
way you think, not in the way the world treats you.*

THE SECRET FORMULA

There was once a scientist, a good and a peaceful man,
who created many useful products. But he lived in a country torn apart by violence. Many times while walking to his
laboratory he was innocently caught up by riots in the
streets. Just to avoid the madness cost him considerable
time and energy. He wondered whether his own scientific
mind could solve the problem.

It did. With careful research, he developed a secret for-
mula which made him invisible. Because rioters could not
see him, he easily passed through the street violence. He
recovered his time and energy.

*These truths make you psychologically invisible, after
which you easily avoid what used to cause trouble.*

THE TAPESTRY

In a city on the Arabian peninsula there was a special
temple. On its walls hung a tapestry of rare beauty. Its in-
genious designs and colors made it an outstanding work of

art. Tradition said it had come from a Sufi school of higher wisdom.

Below the tapestry was printed: FOR THOSE WHO LOVE BEAUTY.

Over the years, the tapestry was viewed by thousands of visitors. All of them went away in agreement that it was truly for those who loved beauty, for everyone felt new emotions while standing before it.

However, a few of the viewers agreed in a different way. Within the tapestry's designs were hidden several symbols which expressed great esoteric truths. People who had developed themselves inwardly could read and understand the symbols. These people loved a higher beauty.

To see wonders unseen by the multitudes on earth, develop your psychic sight.

ACCURATE GUIDES TO DAILY HARMONY

1. Individual consciousness of inner negativity is the total cure for every human sorrow or tragedy.

2. A person who is whole within himself need never make painful and self-dividing decisions.

3. When we are sufficiently tired of getting wrong answers from society we are ready for right answers from our essence.

4. The truly good person is one who has completely dissolved false ideas about himself.

5. The only way on earth to have no conflict with other people is to have no conflict within oneself.

6. There is a section in every man which appreciates the truth, so our task is to release it fully.

7. Freedom from heartache and confusion comes by seeing human nature as it is, not as it appears to be on the surface.

8. You can be fully involved with people on the social level while remaining perfectly free of their negative traits.

9. A man attracts to himself the people and events which correspond with his own actual nature.

10. Regardless of what other people do with their lives, make your life one of constantly expanding light.

Chapter 4

OPEN THE DOOR TO AUTHENTIC HAPPINESS

THE HAPPY FUTURE

A man said to himself, "I am unhappy. However, as soon as my goal is attained I will be happy." He attained his goal, but was just as unhappy as before, so he stated, "When I win my new desire I will be happy." He won his desire, but remained unhappy, so he took his bewilderment to a wise man.

"You deceive yourself," said the sage, "into thinking that mere passage of time can make you happy. *You* are both your present and your future. You never experience anything except what you *are*. Today, change what you are, and your future will be happy, for today and tomorrow are the same."

Banish space and time and you live happily here and now.

SECRETS FOR SUPERIOR SKILL

There was once a great architect whose buildings were the wonders of the land. Few in number, his structures combined strength and beauty in a way rarely seen. One day a delegation came to ask the architect, "May we hear the secrets of your superior skill?"

The architect replied, "Tear down your most honored structure."

The answer was shocking, for everyone knew the most honored structure was an ancient building called the Temple of Progress. The delegation departed, puzzled and frustrated, for they knew that no one would permit the destruction of their most honored building.

One day a thunderous storm tore away part of the foundation of the Temple of Progress. Hidden within the ruins were the secrets of the architect's superior skill.

Astonishingly, man claims he wants happiness, yet clings to the yesterdays which prevent it.

TRUE CONTENTMENT

"Nothing seems more important than to have right values," said Charles, "but we have trouble recognizing gold when we see it."

"The recognition of true values requires daily self-observation. A man must see that the winning of his desires leaves him no more content than he was before."

"I have a small glimpse of this," said Charles. "For instance, once I get what I want I immediately want something else."

"Try to see the difference between actual contentment and the temporary thrill of getting what you want."

"What is the state of a man who sees this?"

"He no longer torments himself. He possesses true contentment."

Acquisition cunningly disguises itself as happiness, but in its falseness it always abandons its unwary victim.

ILLUSION

A seeker asked a teacher, "Why do so many unhappy things happen to me?"

"Will you listen to something you do not want to hear?"
"Yes."
"You are unhappy because you live in illusion."
"What is my greatest illusion?"
"The illusion that you are not living in illusion."
An unaware man is unaware he is unaware, and that is the entire human predicament.

THE EMPEROR'S CHOICE

A wise emperor once sent short notes to five of his ministers. Each note simply asked, "What do you do in your spare time?" Though puzzled by the question, each minister sent his reply:
"I build my financial security."
"I involve myself in many excitements."
"I study to understand the meaning of life."
"I travel to shores and mountains."
"I do little but rest and relax."
Said the emperor to himself, "As my personal advisor I need a mature and inquiring mind. I will select the man who wants to understand life."
The only activities of true value are those which aim at inner transformation.

LOVE

Obviously disturbed by a lecture he had heard, a new student approached an advanced disciple. "The teacher warned us against talking about love," said the beginner with a frown. "He almost rebuked us for using the word love at all. Why?"
"Because people talk most about what they possess the least. He wants us to use honesty as a tool for self-elevation. Do you know what motivates him to talk like this?"
"What?"
"Love."
Love exists in the absence of self-reference, which is far above self-dramatizing words and public appearances.

THE WEIRD PHILOSOPHER

A certain man wanted to become wealthy, but failed. He then decided to develop a shallow but publicly impressive personality, but no one was impressed. In despair, he next decided to become a philosopher. As such, he gave lectures which denounced wealth and shallow personality.

His philosophies became so weird they attracted many people whose minds were already inhabited by weirdness. To the philosopher's delight he soon became wealthy and impressive. "You see," he explained in a modest manner to his enthusiastic followers, "humility attracts heaven's success."

But the number of sleeping pills and tension pills the man secretly consumed was astonishing. He never explained them to his followers. For one thing, he himself could not understand why heaven could make him outwardly successful, but could never make him happy.

A philosophy is worthless unless it makes the philosopher successful in his private life.

SOMETHING TO SEE

Requested Lloyd, "Help us to see something we do not see."

"You do not see that your strength and confidence is illusory. You do not believe that under different circumstances you would behave in a different way than now. For example, someone who considers himself an authoritative public leader will feel lost and lonely when change removes him from public view. This is costly self-deception, for by valuing the artificial you deny yourself the real."

Shock and despair are inevitable as long as we insist upon living in illusions about ourselves.

AT THE BROOK

A good and wise king was strolling through the woods

one day, accompanied by a close friend. While pausing at a brook, they were joined by two strangers who did not recognize the king. During the conversation, the strangers criticized the way the country was ruled, showing hostility and contempt for the king.

The king's friend was about to rebuke their rudeness and foolishness, but the king gently led his friend away. Alone again, the king explained, "What good would have resulted from shocking them awake? You must understand human nature. Of course we could have terrified them by revealing my identity, but I learned long ago that it is evil to put people under fear. No, nothing can be done for those who cannot live without hatred and arrogance. Our task is to be inwardly right. Nothing else matters."

Let others live as they insist upon living, while maintaining your own cosmic course.

THE ACTOR

There was once a skilled actor who played many roles to perfection. During different performances he was a daring adventurer, a handsome lover, a wealthy business executive. He acted so often and so well he finally forgot that they were roles; he believed he actually was the man he portrayed.

So the actor was a confused human being. Whenever meeting an event for which he had no role he felt lost and frightened.

Strangely, he did not see through his roles, even when suffering from them.

Unhappiness always includes role-playing of one kind or another, which means that true happiness has no self-dramatization.

THE INSINCERE SEEKER

A troubled man approached an advanced student of esotericism. The student, who knew an insincere inquirer

when he saw one, saw one, for the student himself was once
on this level.

"Please tell me my faults so I can correct them," requested the troubled man.

"You really do not want to know them," stated the student politely.

The man retorted indignantly, "Of course I want to
know. Otherwise, why would I ask?"

"For two reasons," replied the student. "One of them is
idle curiosity. Secondly, it makes you the center of
the conversation. If I revealed your faults, you might smile,
but you would be secretly angry."

The inquirer smiled and went away angry.

*Sincerity is the first and last requirement for elevating
ourselves above our troubles.*

THE CONTENTED MAN

There was once a man whose irritable nature was
known by all who met him. Nothing pleased him. Everything made him more sour than before. There lurked within the man's mind the suspicion that everyone was intent
on betraying and hurting him.

Quite unexpectedly, a definite change came over the
man. He became patient, undemanding, content. When
asked about the marvelous change he explained, "All my
life I sought something to make me contented. Since it
never came, I decided to be content without it."

*Contentment can never be found by adding anything,
but by resting in our natural wholeness in the here and now.*

SUFFERING MUST BE STUDIED

"Tell us what we need to know about suffering," some
pupils asked their teacher as they sat outdoors in a garden.

The teacher responded, "I wish I could urge you a thousand times to study your very suffering in order to end it.
People use all sorts of tricks to avoid a direct confrontation

with their distress. They invent a phony heaven in the future or escape into distracting excitements." Nodding toward a red rose the teacher explained, "Suffering is like a rose seed planted in the ground. The seed endures the darkness in order to grow up into the sunlight as an entirely new creation."

It is highly intelligent to study suffering scientifically, with an aim to understand, which ends suffering.

PEOPLE IN CONTRADICTION

Mr. and Mrs. T. came for a personal conference with a teacher of esotericism. "Please explain," requested Mr. T., "the contradiction in so-called religious people. Their ways do not match their words."

"Because they know the words, people believe they have had the experience. That is like living on the steps of a mansion instead of in the mansion itself. An awakened man tries to show such people the difference, which is almost always resisted. Those who gain ego-pleasure or other rewards from their exterior form of religion are hostile to true religion. Such people suffer from their contradiction, but neglect to understand and end it."

Man's task is to uplift his inner state to the level of his public preaching.

THE VINE

Students in a group in Chicago were requested to bring an illustration to class. One student contributed:

"Man can be compared to a young vine growing in a shady place. While having power for movement, it needs guidance. Understanding the needs of the vine, the gardener attempts to turn it in the right direction. When yielding to the gardener's higher knowledge, the vine finds itself rising into the sunshine it needs and always wanted."

The student concluded, "Man is a vine in a shady place.

To reach spiritual sunshine, he must yield to higher knowledge, to Reality."

The higher knowledge needed for spiritual sunshine is freely available to those who are weary of shady places.

THE REWARD

A young student at an esoteric school approached his teacher to announce, "I have spent the entire morning improving the garden. What is my reward?"

The teacher inquired, "Are you somewhat worried that you might not get a reward, or that an offered reward might not please you?"

"Yes."

"Tomorrow morning, work once more in the garden. Do it just because you do it, without worrying over a reward. That will be your reward."

Our true reward is to live without demands which cause worry; to simply enjoy our own company at each moment.

THE SPARROW'S COMPLAINT

A sparrow complained to Mother Nature, "You gave beautiful colors to the peacock and a lovely song to the nightingale, but I am plain and unnoticed. Why was I made to suffer?"

"You were not," stated Mother Nature. "You suffer because you make the same foolish mistake as human beings. You *compare*. Be yourself, for in that there is no comparison and no pain."

Comparison operates on the level of conditioned thought, so by transcending thought we never compare and never suffer.

ENCOURAGEMENT

A teacher in Oregon asked his class, "How would you

encourage a gloomy person?" The students replied:

Thomas: "You are never asked to do the impossible, therefore, newness of mind is possible."

Jane: "Limitation of everything truly good for you exists only in an incorrectly operating mind."

Victor: "Things which make a big difference to the false self make no difference whatever to your true nature."

Barbara: "The nice thing about not having an adorable self-image is that you don't have to live up to it."

Owen: "The reason you can begin anew every day is because you *are* new every day."

What you now take as pleasant thoughts for encouragement will someday be seen as scientific facts for self-transformation.

CANDY

Two young men in Syria decided to go into the candy business. Calling on an experienced candymaker in their village, they learned many useful facts. When leaving, one said, "We must first find a source of sugar and buy as much as we can."

His excited friend began to walk away, protesting, "That will take too long. I already have some flour at home. I will use that."

"But you can't substitute flour for sugar."

"You do it your way and I'll do it mine."

When there is a difference between our way and the right way, there is also chaos.

THE TWO BALLOONS

An orange balloon and a blue balloon were set free to float around sky and earth. They separated, but a year later the winds brought them together again. Instantly, the blue balloon began a long story of oppression and misfortune. "I resent getting bumped by everything," the complaint ended.

The orange balloon nodded in understanding. "At first I suffered from the same bumps. Then I learned a fantastic secret which may sound strange to you. I learned to *not enjoy my resentment*. Now, I still run into all sorts of objects, but miraculously, I don't feel a thing. You see, I learned that my resentment *was* the bump."

If we could only see it, we are at the mercy of absolutely nothing except our own wrong thinking.

THE BRACELET

A woman with a careless mind was given a bracelet which she believed to be of great value. She lived in daily worry that it might be stolen or damaged. One day she decided to buy a stronger case to keep it in, so she took it to a jeweler.

Glancing at the bracelet, the jeweler said, "There is no need to protect it from anything. This bracelet has no value at all."

Stunned at first by the news, the woman said nothing. Then she exclaimed, "Thank heaven, my worries are over!"

Worry ends completely for whoever realizes he does not consist of that surface personality which was so anxiously protected.

THE TRAIL TO THE TOP

A national park included a particularly difficult hiking trail which led to the peak of a mountain. Even though long and tiring, it was a favorite with visitors. Those who reached the top did so with a sense of achievement.

Halfway to the top there was an especially steep stretch of twisting trail. Weary hikers who reached this point came upon an unexpected sign. It read: COURAGE! OTHERS HAVE SUCCEEDED!

Simply remember that you can do anything that is necessary for reaching self-recovery.

SUFFERING AND SELF-KNOWLEDGE

A teacher answered these questions:

"From what does a man suffer?"

"From what he does not know about himself."

"What is an example of the kind of knowledge needed?"

"A man must see how he secretly cherishes anguish because it makes him the center of his own attention."

"In summary, how is suffering eliminated?"

"By deep and persistent self-study which leads to self-knowledge."

Ponder the fundamental fact that anguish and understanding cannot occupy the mind at the same time.

STORMY WEATHER

Eva came to her first meetings after suffering the pains of a broken romance. One evening she said, "I know there is something right about everything we hear here, but I seem to be standing in my own way. How can we learn faster?"

"Imagine a highway used by trucks to bring food to a city. The highway cuts across a region having sudden and furious storms which wash out the bridges and block the trucks. That is similar to what happens when we are overwhelmed by stormy emotions, such as bitterness and self-pity. No one cuts us off from swift progress except ourselves. Starting right now, free yourself from negative emotions by refusing their destructive thrill."

Never listen to the false voice which says there is satisfaction in fiery feelings, such as panic and dread.

PERFECT PINEAPPLES

There was once a field of pure and perfect pineapples. The fruit was so superior that the owner never permitted any bargaining over the price, even though bargaining was a popular custom.

All day long the shoppers came to glance at the pine-apples. Most of them used all kinds of cunning tricks to avoid paying the fixed price. But all were told, "There can be no bargaining with such perfect pineapples. Either you want them or you do not."

Many shoppers departed in anger and criticism. But others inspected carefully, and, recognizing perfection, gladly made the purchase.

Truth never bargains, but comes to those who pay the price, the price being a willingness to abandon self-centered ways.

HOW TO USE LIFE

Two students were observing a newcomer to their esoteric school. One morning they saw him trying to drag a water hose to a corner of the garden. But at every few yards the hose caught itself against the stepping stones. Annoyance was plainly on the face of the newcomer as he walked back to loosen the hose.

"Too bad," remarked one student to the other, "but life is using him."

A month later the students again observed the new-comer at the same task. Once more the hose caught against the stepping stones. As the newcomer loosened the hose, a new expression was on his face. Clearly, he was studying his annoyance instead of going along with it.

"Very good," stated a student. "Now he is using life."

An extraordinary secret for true success is to use every annoyance to gain self-insight and self-command.

HELPFUL FACTS ABOUT TRUE HAPPINESS

1. Since the present moment is free of time, you are now free of inner pains, but must realize what this means.

2. Man's entire problem is that he is unaware of being unaware, so self-rescue begins with a new consciousness.

3. Anything that contributes to a deeper understanding of your mind contributes to personal happiness.

4. Authentic love exists in the absence of a fictitious sense of self, and nowhere else.

5. Happiness is present when there is no difference between the inner man and the outer man.

6. Know that contentment is never found by adding anything, but is found by subtracting whatever is artificial and illusory.

7. When suffering is studied and understood through esoteric science, suffering ends for the scientist.

8. No person is ever at the mercy of anything except his own incorrectly operating mind.

9. Never forget that whatever is necessary for self-newness is also possible.

10. Everything works in favor of the person who meets his day with an awakened mind.

Chapter 5

DISCOVER THE MARVELS OF A NEW MIND

BOXES OF SILVER

A ship of the eighteenth century was entering a harbor in Portugal with a rich cargo of silver. It struck an unseen rock and sank in shallow but dark water. Divers tried to tie ropes to the boxes of silver, but were confused by the darkness. The captain realized that the divers were wasting time trying to distinguish between the boxes of silver and the boxes containing products ruined by the water.

"Don't try to judge what you see down there," the captain told his sailors. "Just send everything up to the surface." The divers followed instructions.

In the light of day, the valuable silver was easily separated from worthless boxes.

The light of consciousness enables us to distinguish between true riches and the valueless.

A VANISHING QUESTION

Said a bewildered man to a teacher, "I do not know what to do with myself."

"Understand and correct your mind."

"Will I then know what to do?"

"Yes."

"Then what exactly will I do?"

"You will do everything you do without asking what you should do. The question will vanish. Your mind will no longer be divided against itself. You will *be* what you do, which is self-unity."

To be in agreement with your own nature is all you ever need to be or do.

SOMETHING TO THINK ABOUT

In a class in Toronto, Canada, Bert requested, "Please give us something to think about for the next few days."

"No one is ever really endangered by anything but his own wrong thoughts, his fantasies parading as facts. Think diligently about this. A man free of his own fantasies cannot be threatened by the cunning delusions of others. To reinforce this principle, please restate it in your own words."

Brenda: "Our only enemy is our own mental meandering."

Lowell: "Self-liberty guarantees liberty from the traps of others."

Edith: "Fear of danger vanishes with self-knowledge."

No man is deceived except by his own permission, and the permission is unconscious, for consciousness cannot be deceived.

INSTRUMENTS FOR SEEING

Wishing to teach a certain lesson to her young pupils, a schoolteacher set three objects on her desk. She then asked the children to look at the objects and name them. The students responded:

"A telescope."

"A microscope."

"A magnifying glass."

The teacher asked, "What do they have in common?"
A student answered, "All of them help us to see better."

"That is right. They are instruments for seeing." The teacher applied the lesson, "You must use all your instruments for seeing your lessons, such as attention and effort."

Our instruments for spiritual seeing are ready for today's use, such as verifying everything for oneself, and remembering our high aims.

AT THE PALACE

A disciple asked his teacher, "What is the difference between intelligent thinking and mechanical thinking?" The teacher replied, "Wait a few days."

The next week both men were part of an audience gathered for a public ceremony on palace grounds. In front of them stood a tall man with a glittering crown on his head and dressed in royal robes. Next to him was a shorter man dressed in rags.

Exclaimed the disciple, "What a dazzling crown on the king's head!"

Said the teacher, "The ragged man is the king, who yearly shows his humility. Now you know the difference between intelligent thinking and mechanical thinking. Don't judge from external appearances."

Mechanical thinking, which often makes mistakes, can be corrected by pausing and pondering until all the facts become clear.

THE GLOBE

A student of higher thought worked for a company which manufactured maps and globes. One evening he came to class with a transparent globe of the world. From a pocket he withdrew a small figure of a man with a length of string attached. The student dropped the man through a hole in the top of the globe, holding him suspended in the center of the plastic world.

"This illustrates a good lesson for all of us," stated the student. "There is something wrong with this man. Do you see what it is?"

The student paused a moment, lifted the man out of the globe and explained, "Stop thinking you are the center of the world."

Only in wrong thought do we appear to be the center of the world, which is cured by thinking above ourselves.

THE BEAM OF LIGHT

Two friends were walking home on a dark night, when one of them turned his flashlight upward. "What a magical feat if we could walk upward on that beam of light," he remarked.

"An interesting but foolish idea," replied his friend.

"But think about it. If you could walk up that beam of light you would be the most famous man on earth."

"I would be a sensation all right," agreed the other man.

"You have nothing to lose by trying it," said the man with the flashlight. "Go ahead. Try to walk up that beam of light."

"You can't trick me," said his friend with a cunning smile. "The moment I reach the top you'll turn it off."

Constant association with foolish ideas will make a man foolish.

THE INTERVAL

Arnold's office was close to the meeting place. Arriving early one evening, he said, "Right responses seem to be of utmost importance. Will you discuss it, please."

"Thoughts rush through the mind one after another like cars of a speeding train. But by watching you can detect an interval between them. Mental clearness and a right response exist within this interval. By resting in this interval you prevent impulsive and harmful responses from crashing through. Practice this seeing and resting. It slows down thought, and the interval becomes clear, just as you see between two train cars to the land beyond."

Realize the difference between thinking with mechanical memory and seeing with your total nature.

THE TWO FISH

Two fish met in the Atlantic Ocean. The first fish said he came from a part of the sea inhabited by savage sharks. He spent a half-hour describing his dangers and hardships. Several times he mentioned his heroic service in saving other fish from sharks. "I don't wish to appear immodest," the first fish concluded, "but I suppose you could call me a suffering hero."

The second fish came from a safe and quiet part of the ocean, which he described to the other fish. He added, "There is no need for heroics there, for no one ever attacks anyone else. Follow me and I will show you this peaceful place."

"Don't be foolish," exclaimed the first fish as he swam away. "It isn't every day you meet a suffering hero."

People prefer their vanity-based imaginations about themselves over reality and peace.

THE TIME

A church official in a small town frequently phoned the city hall to ask for the correct time. One day while visiting the city hall he paused to thank the young woman who had helped him. He explained, "Your information enables me to ring the church bell exactly on time."

She replied, "How strange. I listen to the bell to set *my* time."

One dependent man foolishly follows another dependent man, and both fall into the ditch.

THE REVOLVING WHEEL

A man sought directions to a new colony where he wanted to live. After considerable search he contacted an advisor who knew all about the colony. The advisor explained, "There are directions to the colony, but they require patience and endurance. Inside a temple not far from here there is a revolving wheel. The directions are printed on the wheel, so, of course, you cannot read them until the wheel slows down. Since it takes time for the wheel to lose speed, are you willing to patiently wait until it happens?"

The advisor saw that this man did indeed have the needed patience, for he came back with the directions.

A patient study of one's nervously revolving mind
slows it down to where its accurate directions can be read.

THE DINNER

There was once a man who had the foolish habit of hypnotizing himself. Refusing to face reality, he habitually escaped his anxiety by falling under a self-induced trance. One evening he entered a restaurant and ordered a full dinner. While waiting to be served he felt disturbed by something and so sought relief by hypnotizing himself.

While still under hypnosis, he ate his dinner. He awakened just as he finished. Looking down at the empty plates he called with annoyance to the waiter. "What kind of service is this? I asked for a full dinner and this is what you give me."

People dwelling under spiritual self-hypnosis cannot recognize higher truth when it is served to them.

RIGHT THINKING

A study group in Scotland expressed these ideas about right thinking:

"Only when losing something of value, and taking that loss rightly, can we begin to recognize true value."

"To know what you want is not the same as knowing what is beneficial."

"Anything from which a man runs is never anyplace but within the runner."

"Consider the possibility that others may see you in an entirely different way than you see yourself."

"The only way to learn to distinguish between right and wrong is to prefer right to wrong."

"The man who makes it is the man who sees there is really no other way than forward."

Realize every day that a rightly operating mind will make that day what you wish it to be.

THE DESERT TORTOISE

While flying over the desert, a sea gull paused to rest on a rock. A desert tortoise came along to state, "I have never seen a bird like you before. Where are you from?"

The sea gull described the ocean, mentioning its main features, including its enormous size and its waves.

As the sea gull flew away, the tortoise went home to tell his wife about the conversation. "At first I thought that bird had something new," said the tortoise, "but then I saw that we have the same things. It is simply a matter of words. What he calls the ocean we call the desert. What he calls water we call sand. Guess there is nothing really new in the world."

A closed mind interprets everything according to its own familiar thinking habits.

THE COIN IN THE POND

A man was seated beside a pond when he accidentally dropped a coin into the water. He poked around with a stick in an attempt to separate the coin from the stones. But this stirred up so much mud he could see nothing.

Not knowing what else to do, he sat quietly for awhile. Then, glancing down, he saw clear water again. He also saw his coin.

An agitated mind can never find the answers which belong to a settled and quiet mind.

THE MAYOR

A teacher of higher truth wished to correct the thinking habits of his students. He asked two of them, "What is the character of the mayor of this village?"

Replied one student, "He is a wonderful man."

Answered the other pupil, "He is a terrible tyrant."

"What both of you really mean," said the teacher, "is that *you think* he is either wonderful or terrible. Why do you have opposite opinions? Because you base them on self-interest. For example, he either gave or denied you something you wanted. You did not describe the mayor at all; you described your own attitudes. Be clear in your own mind and you will clearly and wisely see the mayor, whatever he may be."

Where there is no false self with its false interests, everyone and everything is seen with practical clarity.

THE DIZZY WORLD

Three friends were strolling through the countryside. Suddenly, all three slipped and fell into a ditch, striking their heads lightly.

Rising, one man glanced out to yell in terror, "Look! The world is spinning dizzily!"

"Horrible!" cried another. "We must make plans to stop its mad whirl."

The pair ran off to get help.

The third man pondered, "I wonder where this dizziness exists?"

When the mind ceases to whirl with illusion, the world stops spinning.

THE THIRD WAY OF THINKING

During an informal discussion after a class, Roger said, "I finally saw the mistake I had made for years. When hearing an argument of any kind, perhaps political or religious, I thought one side was right and the other side wrong." Roger paused to smile. "Of course it was always *my* side that was right. Now I know that both sides were wrong, for argument is a nervous attempt to make wrong seem right."

Roger continued, "There is a third way of thinking

which is above two opposing sides. However, the unenlight-
ened mind is unable to conceive it as long as the individual
insists upon clinging to illusion. But any sincere person can
live from the third way of thinking. In its clear consciousness is sanity and happiness."

*The third way of thinking, which is above this side and
that side, is a wondrous state of mind.*

SECRET THOUGHTS

A teacher said to a nervous and confused inquirer, "You
understand neither yourself nor life." The inquirer nodded
and replied, "You are probably right." But the inquirer's
mind secretly exploded with, "What right do you have to in-
sinuate that I lack understanding?"

The teacher continued, "You must stop wasting your
life." Answered the inquirer, "I would like to stop all
right." But the inquirer resentfully thought, "How rude of
you to say that I have not lived intelligently and constructively."

The teacher stated, "You can begin right now to find
true peace of mind." The inquirer assured the teacher,
"That is what I want above all else." But a corner of the inquirer's mind rejoiced, "I am glad I discovered what a danger this man is to my peace of mind."

*Those who pretend to want the truth are like a thirsty
man who throws away a cup of pure water.*

THE YARDSTICK

A native of a primitive tribe in South America was given
a ruler one foot long. He found great pleasure going around
measuring everything by his ruler. He discovered that his
hand was seven inches long, and that his eating bowl was
twelve inches wide.

But he did not know how to measure anything which was
longer than twelve inches. The length of his ruler was the
limit of his comprehension.

One day he was given a yardstick. He was greatly astonished to discover that he could measure objects longer than twelve inches.

Never believe that the limit of comprehension is the limit of life.

THE MAN WHO FELT OWED

A wise man asked a man with a muddled mind, "Do you feel you have the right to make demands on another person?"

"Yes."

"Does he have the same right to make demands on you?"

"No."

"Why not?"

"Because he owes me something."

"But he thinks you owe something to him."

"He is a self-centered man with no love for justice."

"There is a totally new way to see life, in which you neither owe nor are owed."

A healthy and untroubled mind does not dwell in the opposing states of feeling owed or of guiltily òwing.

LILLIAN'S LETTERS

Lillian, who attended classes regularly, had a personal experience with something she had learned at the meetings.

As a secretary, she once typed dozens of letters, dating them with the correct month of January. On the first day of February she caught herself still typing the month of January.

She reflected, "That is what we learned last week. The mechanical part of the mind lingers in yesterday. Therefore, it can't meet today correctly. I will handle today with today's newness."

A mind operating in the present moment only is free of yesterday's interference, and therefore operates perfectly.

SIMPLE LOGIC

A man with many conflicts was asked, "What do you believe to be the source of your many troubles?"

The man replied instantly, "I am always right and others are always wrong. But others will never admit I am right and they are wrong."

"Skipping the enormous egotism of that statement, let's look at it from the viewpoint of simple logic. How is it possible for you to always be right and for others to always be wrong?"

"That," exclaimed the man with a dramatic sigh, "is one of the great miracles of the ages."

Logic cannot penetrate vanity.

WILD CARGO

A ship entered a port in Africa to seek a cargo for the return trip to Europe. Having some personal business ashore, the captain assigned the details of the cargo to his officers. Returning to the ship late one night, the captain gave orders to sail.

The next morning the captain heard strange noises below deck. Going down, the noises turned into fierce roars and screaming voices. Glancing around, the captain saw several lions chasing around the cages from which they had escaped. Taking instant command, the captain directed the crew in returning the lions to their cages.

Realizing his carelessness, the captain said to himself, "Next time I will check my cargo personally."

Check your mental cargo of beliefs and attitudes.

THE KIND OF WORLD

A young squirrel and an equally young chipmunk became friends when meeting at the base of a tree. "Let's see what kind of world we inhabit," suggested the squirrel. The chipmunk agreed.

Climbing the tree, they called to each other from different branches. Announced the squirrel, "The world is beautiful with sparkling streams and sunny hills."

"No," denied the chipmunk. "It is a world of pale grass and nothing else."

"Ah!" exclaimed the squirrel. "I see the problem. I am on the top branch and you are on the lowest. Come on up!"

Elevate the viewpoint and we elevate the world, for our world consists of our viewpoint.

PLANS FOR WINNING NEWNESS OF MIND

1. Constantly develop your talent for distinguishing between the valuable and the useless.

2. Prove all these principles for yourself, which you are quite capable of doing.

3. There is a quiet space between rushing thoughts in which all is seen clearly and in which everything becomes right.

4. The very realization that a nervous mind can accomplish nothing worthwhile can end nervousness in life.

5. Take every loss or defeat with a mind which wants to know life's answers, and the loss turns into gain.

6. The world you experience exists in your mind, so change your world by changing your mind.

7. Thinking with awareness and intelligence is to think above opposing positions taken by battling human beings.

8. Never accept your present world as the only kind of world which exists for you.

9. Yesterday's mistakes have no power whatever to interfere with today's right performances.

10. Today, challenge a belief or opinion, to see whether it produces the kind of life you really want.

Chapter 6

HOW TO CURE DAILY DIFFICULTIES SWIFTLY

THE BUSINESSMAN'S SUCCESS

A businessman in earnest about inner transformation developed his own method for meeting daily events correctly. He pictured himself standing at the base of a sloping hill. He then pictured a ball rolling down the hill, which could bounce into a weedy field at his left, or into a box on his right. Everything depended upon his handling of the ball when it reached him. It could be lost in the weeds or saved and used.

It was excellent self-help. Among other things, he learned to meet an event with a new and clear mind. Then, an event remained an *event*, and never turned into a *problem*.

Each day we receive hundreds of impressions from the external world, which can be used for constructive self-change, or which can be wasted.

THE MOST IMPORTANT FACT

Two students of higher knowledge had an excellent intention. They were determined to let daily experiences teach them spiritual lessons. They were strolling through

the woods one day when one of them shouted, "Look out!
A pit!" Both leaped aside in time to avoid falling into a pit
covered by vines.

"What was the most important fact about that pit?"
one asked the other.

"The fact that someone carelessly left a danger like
that?"

"No."

"The fact that we nimbly jumped aside?"

"No."

"What, then?"

"The fact that we *saw* it."

*One thing alone delivers us from daily injury, and that
is an awareness of a pit as a pit.*

INWARD INVESTIGATION

Edwin, a government employee, asked, "What do you
mean by solving a difficulty with inward investigation?"

"Suppose you feel mistreated by someone. Glance inward. Notice your boiling feelings. Who is boiling and
therefore who is punished by it? You. See how you mistreat
yourself. Really see it. You will realize that what you
thought was exterior mistreatment is really mistreatment
of yourself by yourself. Your awareness of this is liberty,
for no man consciously injures himself."

*The inward look is the only cure for an exterior diffi-
culty, for the problem is not out there, but in here.*

GET THE FACTS

"When something goes wrong, get the facts." That was
a teacher's advice to his followers as he departed on a trip.

Three days later, with the teacher still absent, some of
the students needed to get the facts. One was upset because
his work on the school grounds had been criticized. Another
felt mistreated when he was not allowed to talk at great
length about his personal difficulties. Seeking the facts,

the students found just what they needed in the teacher's notebook, which read:

1. *When jolted by anything it simply means you are dwelling out of harmony with your true nature. It means you are asleep, while dreaming you are awake.*

2. *However, you can use every jolt for self-awakening. Just let it destroy an illusion or a vanity.*

To awaken from mental sleep you must first understand what it means to be asleep, which is promoted by your present reading.

THE SUPERIOR GRAPES

A city dweller became the guest of a country friend who who had a large field of grapes. Host and guest took a stroll through the field. Selecting a grape of an unusual color, the host said, "This is a new and superior grape. Try it." Tasting the grape, the guest's lips twisted. "I'm afraid it's sour," he politely remarked.

Over the next few days the host repeatedly invited his friend to taste the unusual grape. The guest reluctantly agreed.

Later, when departing, the guest remarked, "You know, that grape was sour at first, but grew sweeter with each taste."

The host smiled. "I know. That is part of its uniqueness."

Higher facts are untasty to our old and habitual nature, but become delicious as our new nature grows stronger.

HOW TO MAKE LIFE EASIER

A teacher and his students were driving through livestock country. "Notice," said the teacher, "how an animal mingles with its own kind. Cows mix with cows, sheep with sheep. Do you see how this law applies to human behavior?"

When the students shook their heads, the teacher con-

tinued, "You attract people and circumstances which correspond with your own nature, your own level of being.
You attract what you are."

Someone asked, "Could an understanding of this make
our lives easier?"

"Certainly. It will awaken the energy necessary for
raising your level of being. To attract something different
you must change what you are. A new consciousness attracts new conditions effortlessly."

*The one way to change outer conditions is to change the
inner condition.*

HELEN'S PROBLEM

Asked Helen, a new member of the class, "Can these
teachings aid us in everyday matters?"

"Do you have a specific problem in mind?"

Helen laughed. "It's a constant problem to me. Can I be
helped in ending shyness, as when meeting people for the
first time?"

"Unfortunately, people never see how practical we are,
here. Of course you can change. What is shyness? You may
not understand as yet, but it is a defense of imaginary ideas
we have about ourselves. As imagination ends, so does defense and shyness. Try to grasp this much for now. You
will see."

*Think of the relief you will have when you no longer
protect that which needs no protection.*

THE HIGHER ANSWER

A schoolteacher wished to teach his young pupils to
think from higher positions, so he arranged a visual lesson.
Writing the answer to a question in science on a slip of
paper he placed it on a shelf which was above the heads of
the students. One at a time he asked two boys and two girls
to reach for the answer, which they did.

"Remember," the teacher made his point, "that the

answer to a question resides on a level above your present level. Learn to reach above yourself.''

Upon the appearance of a problem we must remember that the true answer dwells above the level of the conditioned mind.

A TEACHING ABOUT SECURITY

A sparrow flew in and out of several trees in an orchard, seeking a secure place for its nest. Selecting a tree, it began to build on one of the higher branches. Noticing the sparrow's first trips, the orchardist scattered the bits which were forming the nest. Undiscouraged, the sparrow selected another tree and began a second nest, but it was also scattered by the orchardist. The sparrow then began work in a tree which grew close to the orchardist's home. Nodding in satisfaction, the orchardist watched with interest as the sparrow completed its nest.

A few days later the orchardist cut down the trees selected originally by the sparrow. They had become too weak to withstand strong winds.

Though the sparrow did not understand, the orchardist did.

When our search for security is frustrated, we need only understand the whole process of life.

THE SECRET OF THE AGES

An inquirer asked a teacher, "How can I command whatever happens to me?"

"By being one with whatever happens."

"What does that mean?"

"You really do not possess a separate self which is apart from anything; you are one with all of life. However, in your misunderstanding you think there is a you *and* an event, which causes division and conflict. Give up your belief in a separate self and oneness will be realized, which ends conflict. This is the secret of the ages. Come back to it every day. You will change."

You become the commander of everything by not needing to command anything but yourself.

HOW TO END SELF-INJURY

Mr. and Mrs. D. wanted to know, "What causes false and therefore self-damaging conclusions?"

"They are caused by taking the part as the whole. Suppose you see the wind bend a tree toward the west. You conclude that the sky has a westward wind. However, at a higher level in the same sky the wind may be blowing east or north or south. So it is the entire sky which is vital, for its winds are interrelated. A man may pretend to respect the existence of other people, but his egotism secretly believes only in itself. Seeing the whole of life—really seeing it—ends self-harming conclusions."

Errors of judgment occur when one part of the mind wrongly assumes it is the whole mind, thus blocking whole perception.

THE COUNTRY WOMAN

There was once a very lonely woman who lived alone in the forest. Every day she set out bits of food for the wild animals who came around. The animals seemed to like her, which made her feel better.

But one day she ran short of food, so the animals stopped coming around. Her loneliness returned more hurtful than before.

However, the woman had once read a book which said, "Dependency causes anxiety. Don't find fickle friends. Find yourself."

So the woman found herself and was never again lonely.

When wisely used, disappointment enables comprehension to replace inner hauntings.

THE INVENTOR

An inventor was baffled by a problem connected with a machine he was creating. Certain wheels failed to function as desired. He decided to seek assistance from a scientist who had superior knowledge of such things.

For an hour the inventor talked about the problem to the scientist, then talked another hour about possible solutions. When he finally stopped talking he was made uneasy by the silence of the scientist. Somewhat timidly he asked, "When may I expect your help?"

"When you run out of solutions."

Solutions to life's problems can reach us only when we no longer assume we already have them.

THE CLOCK

A man once owned a large and expensive clock, made by skilled craftsmen in Switzerland. He kept the clock in a window, where it was seen by passersby who set their watches by it.

But something was wrong with the clock. Its hands habitually showed the wrong time. So the man spent considerable energy every day in turning the clock's hands to the right positions.

This went on for several years, which kept the owner weary. One day someone suggested, "Instead of wasting your energy in correcting the hands, why don't you fix the clock's inner parts?"

"What a tremendous idea!" the owner exclaimed in astonishment and delight. "I never thought of that!"

People seldom think of changing their inner nature for the purpose of ending useless and tiring daily tasks.

HOW TO MAKE EVERYTHING DIFFERENT

When problems were discussed in class, Nancy threw up her arms to exclaim, "But how can we find all the needed solutions?"

"Place all your problems in one basket. They might consist of worry, overweight, regret, problems connected with sex. They are now in front of you. Now realize that each problem does not have a separate cause, not at all. There is but one underlying cause of all the problems. It is the false belief of having a separate ego. Go on from there. How would things be different if you lived from the Whole, and not from a sense of separation? You would never fear the loss of your sex partner, you would never feel inferior when others win more money or popularity than you. Think along these lines."

When you are truly different, everything else is astonishingly different.

WHAT TO DO

A student of higher truth brought a friend to a lecture. While waiting for the talk to begin the student said, "The teacher not only knows the answers but knows all the questions. You will see."

The student was right, for the lecture began, "You constantly ask what you should do. This is what everyone asks. What should you do? There is only one answer. You must permit truth to bring you an understanding of yourself and your life. But many of you wrongly assume you already understand. Others run away because it sounds too difficult or too mysterious. Remember that right doing always involves an effort to gain new knowledge. Do this and the question of what to do will fade away."

You will be pleased at how perplexing questions fade away in the light of cosmic knowledge.

CORRECT STEPS

Two friends regularly exchanged helpful plans for attaining the new life. One evening one of them gave the other a slip of paper which read:

To not get hurt by others you must understand them.

To do this you must first understand yourself.

To do this you must see yourself as you really are.

To do this you must examine yourself honestly and constantly.

To do this you must have a deep wish for the new life.

Your life unfolds according to what you accept as true about yourself, so self-facts are all-important.

ESCAPE PLANS

The following plans for escaping psychic imprisonment were offered by a study group in Tennessee:

"It is both courageous and necessary for us to see that we do not understand many things we assume we understand."

"I cannot change my psychological atmosphere without first changing the way I think, for my thoughts *are* my atmosphere."

"A wise man changes causes, while a foolish man merely rearranges effects."

"It took steady work but I finally saw that no true benefit could ever come from trying to win the favor of other people."

"To see a situation with mental health is to see it freshly, without the interference of conditioned thought."

Connect these escape plans with a condition in your own life, using them to change that condition, for you can succeed.

THE WOOL COAT

There was once a merchant who believed himself possessed of superior judgment. One day, wanting a new coat, he went into the country and selected one particular sheep out of a flock. "Get wool from that sheep only," he instructed the shepherd, "and have your local tailor make me a new coat."

When the coat was delivered the merchant was proud of

its style and comfort. He credited its success to his own judgment in selecting that particular sheep.

A week later he met the shepherd who explained he had been unable to use the selected sheep. When hearing this the merchant felt depressed and angry.

In the absence of human vanity, daily circumstances cannot cause distress.

FACTS ABOUT UNHAPPY RESULTS

Asked Bruce, "Why do so many unhappy results come my way?"

"There are two explanations. Firstly, they happen because you do not understand cause and effect. You set an unconscious cause into motion, making an unhappy result inevitable. The cause was negative, such as a gloomy feeling, which then attracted its own nature, such as meeting a treacherous person while attempting to escape your gloom. Secondly, to ask *why* something happens means you permit the ego to fight an event instead of letting right thoughts understand the cause of the event. You do not ask why the sun rises because your ego is not involved. Understand yourself and *why* no longer arises."

That we reap what we sow is not just religious sentiment, but a scientific fact we prove every day by our experiences.

THE HYPNOTIZED MAN

An evil magician hypnotized a man, telling him, "You are a great and powerful conqueror. Go into the world and win what is rightfully yours."

Under the influence of the self-picture suggested by the evil magician, the man went out and tried to conquer the world. But all he received was tension and rage and bitterness.

Suspecting something wrong, he worked on himself until he snapped the hypnotic trance with its false self-picture.

All his troubles ended.

All difficulties are caused by psychic hypnosis, and all difficulties are cured by self-awakening.

RISING AND FALLING FORTUNES

Some students in an outdoor class had difficulty grasping the lesson, "You can live in psychological independence of rising and falling exterior fortunes."

The teacher explained, "You are hurt by exterior events because you falsely believe you possess an individual ego which is apart from all of life. You wrongly assume there is a self *and* an event, which causes conflict."

Picking up a stone, the teacher tossed it into the air and let it fall. "Did either the rising or falling hurt the stone? No, for it had no false ego which thought the rising was good but the falling was bad."

When winning the higher victory you have nothing to win or lose on the everyday level of life.

THE MOUNTAINEERS

A club composed of mountain climbers met for dinner. Afterward, they discussed their plans for the first climb of the season.

"The first thing I intend to do," said one of them, "is to find a new peak to conquer."

"My first act," said another, "will be to inform the newspapers of my expeditions."

The last man to speak was the most skilled and successful mountaineer in the entire group. He told the others, "I will do the first thing I always do. I will inspect my ropes."

It is strange how human beings seldom inspect the ideas which produce the kind of life they have.

THE PROBLEM OF IDENTITY

Said Virgil, "I am troubled by my lack of identity. I try to tell myself who I am but never succeed."

"When you try to tell yourself who you are, exactly what do you do? Just one thing. You call up memory. Memory says you were the winner of an award last year, you are a social success or a social failure, and so on. Without memory you would not exist in this way, which is a tremendous fact. You are not who memory says you are, for that is merely a cluster of old thoughts, which is certainly not you. Do not use memory to identify yourself, for then you flow freely in the present moment. When a memorized image of yourself does not interfere with right now, right now is peace and liberty."

Discover who you are not—and you are not your collected self-descriptions—and life flows smoothly at last.

SECRET PROTECTION

A secretary lived in a home overlooking a lake. As a hobby she studied the habits of the ducks which visited the lake. One observation puzzled her. When going to sleep on the water the ducks never drifted to shore on the gentle current, which would have been natural. Something in the birds seem to protect them from the dangers in drifting shoreward.

But what? The secretary investigated until the secret was revealed. While tucking one foot up among the feathers, a duck's other foot gave an occasional push in the water, which made it revolve in a circle. Even when appearing unalert, one part of the duck was awake and protective.

Regardless of our many daily involvements, one inner part can remain awake to keep us in the right position.

TRUTHS TO REMEMBER FROM THIS CHAPTER

1. Your daily experiences and impressions can be healthy medicine if used as such.

2. Work inwardly, for that is the source of both the problem and the solution.

3. Stick with a healing truth you do not want to hear, and eventually you will want to hear it.

4. Great relief and relaxation come to everyone who no longer protects imaginary ideas about himself.

5. Remember that an answer to a difficulty resides at a higher level than our usual thinking, so seek this loftier level.

6. Command yourself and you will be in calm command of everything else.

7. Realize that a false sense of self is the cause of all distress and you wash away all distress.

8. Examine the ideas you have about yourself, then make correction according to these principles.

9. Daily events are powerless to disturb the person who lives from his real nature, so discover this nature.

10. Apply the lessons of this chapter to a particular problem or situation in your day.

Chapter 7

THE MIRACLE OF EASY AND NATURAL LIVING

THE CIRCLE

There was once a man who liked to take walks, but was unhappy with them. He complained to a friend, "I fall into bogs and am bitten by insects. Why can't I find a pleasant place to walk?"

His friend replied, "Because you always walk in the same circle."

"Nonsense!" exploded the walker. "I take new routes every day."

"Then how come you always meet the same troubles? Oh, no, you walk in a circle while pretending it is a new place."

"There is some logic in what you say," admitted the walker. "How can I stroll through fresh countryside?"

"Stop loving that familiar circle. Have the courage to step out of it."

Man is so fond of the familiar and the habitual, he refuses to step out of it into his rightful place.

THE REAL REASON

A family was camping in the woods for a few days. One

evening the fifteen-year old son set out for a nearby village to buy some groceries. He returned an hour later with scratched arms and legs. When questioned by his sister he replied, "The reason? In the darkness I walked off the trail into some bushes."

His father commented, "The real reason is because you forgot something. The next time remember to take your flashlight, and all will be well."

We have forgotten our original nature, but when remembered, all is well.

SECRET CODES

Browsing through a shop which sold used books, a customer found a book he had sought for many years. The volume revealed simple methods for solving and understanding secret codes.

When the customer returned to the bookstore a week later, the manager asked whether the book had lived up to expectations. "Yes," answered the customer. "I just had to remove what was not supposed to be in there." He explained that the previous owner had filled the book with scribbled notes, many of them containing erroneous information.

By removing what is not supposed to be within, including feelings of hopelessness, we read and understand the secret codes about life.

THE NEW VIEW

While seeking a site for a new home, a man finally chose a hill overlooking a dry river bed. His friends thought him very foolish. "Your only view is sand and dryness," they told him.

But the man knew something his friends did not know.

One afternoon a trickle of water appeared in the river bed. By evening a clear and attractive stream flowed below the building site.

The man explained to his friends, "It was dry only because the upstream water had been drained away by broken river banks. I bought the property up there and stopped the drainage."

Cosmic wholeness ends the drain of our natural energies, giving us a new view of life.

LET LIFE FLOW

Mr. and Mrs. B. said they were studying the principle of noninterference with the natural flow of life. "Eastern religions teach this," commented Mr. B. "Would you please add to our knowledge?"

"It is the surface personality, the conditioned mind, which anxiously interferes with the natural flow. Suppose you lose something you had depended upon for feeling safe and supported. In itself this loss cannot cause distress. But you are so closely involved with this exterior object that you wrongly conclude you are losing part of yourself. If you did not care whether or not you lost it, there would be no anxiety. This proves that your thinking determines your feelings, not the exterior object. Let life flow as it wishes, without self-interference. Watch what happens."

Everything is met correctly and calmly when met without the anxious interference of surface personality, of self-centered thought.

THE STARS

The father of a small boy studied astronomy in his home. He had a telescope through which he observed the stars every evening. From time to time his son was shown how to look through the telescope. Though not understanding what he saw, the boy sensed that the stars were different from anything he had ever seen before.

One evening the father placed a protective covering over the telescope. Entering the room and not seeing the telescope's familiar shape, the boy's mind went by mental association to the stars he had seen. He asked his father

where the stars had gone. The father uncovered the telescope and showed him that the stars were still there.

*Covering ourselves with faulty ideas does not extinguish
our essence, but we have considerable uncovering to do.*

TRUE SPIRITUALITY

"Like almost everyone else," said a man to a teacher,
"I do not know what it means to be spiritual. Everything
I try is either artificial or impossible."

Said the teacher, "To be truly spiritual means to be
aware of what you are doing at the moment you are doing
it. It means to feel yourself in action at the precise second
of that action."

"But is this awareness possible for me?"

"You could have been aware of yourself asking that
question."

*Artificiality is a result of unawareness, unconsciousness;
so expanding awareness leads to genuine spirituality.*

THE POWER OF REFUSAL

A certain country was ruled by a tyrant who had a nervous affliction. His eyes blinked frantically all day long.
Embarrassed by it, he sought a cure, but found none. So he
issued a decree which commanded everyone to blink their
eyes as he did. Disobedience would bring swift punishment.

So the citizens began to blink as commanded. At first it
felt strange, but it soon became an unconscious habit. Since
their eyes were shut half the time, they often stumbled and
injured themselves. But they rarely questioned the cause
of their pains.

One day a stranger entered the country. He realized at
once that the custom was both ridiculous and dangerous.
He refused to go along with it. And he also refused to
remain in that country.

*You must be firmly convinced that society is not going
to change its ways, which supplies fresh energy for individual change.*

CANARY AND NIGHTINGALE

A man owned a canary which was unable to sing. Wishing to draw out the bird's natural talent, the man placed a nightingale in its cage. He hoped the association of the canary with the melodious nightingale would help.

The nightingale sang beautifully, but the canary remained sadly silent. The owner knew why. The canary had been mistreated by its former owner, which had suppressed its natural talent for song.

Patiently and gently, the owner encouraged the canary. One day it burst forth with a song as beautiful as that of the nightingale. The owner knew what had happened. The canary's original nature had finally overcome its suppression.

By associating only with what is right within us, whatever is wrong is overcome.

THE TRUE AND THE FALSE

Richard asked, "How can we tell whether someone is giving us true spiritual facts or not?"

"If someone tells you he can speak Arabic, how can you test him?"

"Ask him to speak Arabic."

"But how would you know whether he is actually doing so?"

"I would have to know at least a bit of Arabic myself."

"Exactly. To receive the true instead of the false you must first be able to distinguish between them. Many people remain in spiritual immaturity because they insist they already know the difference. They say they are on the inside looking out, but their feelings don't agree. Get the taste of truth through individual effort, after which you can rightly judge the words of others."

Your own recovered naturalness is the perfect judge as to what is true and what is untrue.

THE PEARLS

A pearl diver on an island in the South Pacific brought home a basket of oysters. His young son, who had recently learned about pearls, eagerly opened several oysters, but found no pearls.

The father explained to the disappointed boy, "Not all oysters contain pearls. You must examine each one carefully. Don't hope for a pearl—just examine—and all will be right."

Examine every teaching offered you to see whether it agrees with the truth known by your inner nature.

AN INCREDIBLE FACT ABOUT MAN

A teacher held an empty jar before his class and asked, "What is in here?"

"Nothing."

The teacher wrapped a band of paper around the jar. On the band was the printed label: *SILVER.*

"Now what is in the jar?" the teacher asked.

"Nothing."

"But it is labeled as silver."

"It is as empty as before."

The lesson was taught, "An incredible fact about man is his belief in the reality of mere labels, mere words. He thinks he actually becomes what he *calls* himself. Abolish labels. Be real."

Labels separate a man from himself, so by dropping labels he ends self-division and self-conflict.

THE WILD HORSE

A wild horse roamed the fields and hills according to his own pleasure. On one occasion he wandered over to a pasture where a tame horse was grazing. The tame horse immediately began a conversation, telling the wild horse about the advantages of being owned by a master. "In ex-

change for carrying a man on my back," explained the
tame horse, "I get food and shelter and whatever care I
need. Never do I have to think for myself. I wonder why you
do not join me in this carefree life."

"I wonder why you try so hard to convince me," said the
wild horse as he galloped away.

*Dependence upon others may appear to have advantages,
but our real nature never consents to it.*

THE MAN WHO ADVISED HIMSELF

A man was very successful in his career and very perplexed in his private life. Seeking answers, he visited a
bookstore. To his surprise, he met other customers who
were also seeking solutions. Some of them were very
liberal in giving advice: "Read this popular book," urged
one of them. "Try this exciting volume," said another.

The advice seemed artificial to the man, for the faces
of his advisors revealed that they were also bewildered. So
searching the shelves on his own, he found a book which
emphasized: "Be the person you truly are."

Reflected the man, "This is the book I tell myself I
want."

And that was the book which cleared his perplexity.

*When hearing advice from your own recovered essence
you know exactly what to do.*

THE ACORN

An acorn anxiously asked its mother, a large oak tree,
"How can I become an oak tree like you?"

"Just be yourself," answered the mother.

"But how do I do that?"

"You don't have to do anything but realize your true nature. The moment you try to do anything else you separate
yourself from yourself."

"Sometimes I wish I were a sycamore or cypress tree."

"That is the problem. You are wishing instead of understanding, which causes self-conflict."

"I still don't understand how I can simply be myself."

"Get tired of not being yourself."

Realize that you are never really anyone but yourself, which is a truth that makes you free.

THE BOY AND THE POND

Every morning while walking to school a boy passed a frozen pond. Scattered over the surface of the ice were several rocks, ranging in size from large to small. Also caught by the frozen ice were pieces of wood of various shapes.

As warmer weather gradually thawed the ice, the boy's interest was caught by the changing scene. The rocks slowly sank deeper and deeper into the melting ice until disappearing altogether. But when the pieces of wood were freed by the ice they remained in sight by floating on the water.

Fascinated by nature's changes, the boy remembered the scene over the years. As an adult he reflected, "The very nature of the wood let it float, regardless of changing weather. I will let my own true nature serve in the same way."

Live within the One Nature and you will remain lightly afloat throughout exterior changes.

THE PIGEON

Once there was a pigeon that flew with an average flock of other pigeons. One day in the natural course of events he became separated from the others. He sadly complained, "I wonder why they don't like me?"

On another day he found himself at the head of the flying flock. This made him boast, "What a great leader I am!"

On a third occasion he naturally flew in an opposite direction than the others. He stated firmly, "Everyone is flying in the wrong direction but me."

The pigeon did not see how every natural event was distorted by his misunderstanding and vanity. A wiser pigeon in the same flock saw what was happening and reflected, "I wonder whether I will ever be able to tell him the truth?"

The self-liberated person does not see himself as either the victim or the beneficiary of natural events.

NATURAL RELIGION

There was once a man who wanted to exchange his life of defeat and despair for a life of true triumph. Accordingly, he studied the offered religions, ranging from Religion A to Religion Z. But it left him more confused than before. He still did not know the difference between right and wrong religion.

He was helped by a clear-minded man who told him, "No collection of man-made doctrines can ever be wholly right. For example, some of the religions you studied taught self-reliance. That is right. But the same religions mistake ego-serving sentimentality for love, which is disastrous. Within you is a Natural Religion which is totally correct. I will tell you about it. Remember, this Natural Religion confirms itself, so you never need to take the word of an external teacher."

The wholly correct judgment dwelling within every man reveals itself as swiftly as he casts aside man-made judgments.

HELPFUL STATEMENTS

These helpful statements were made by members of a class in Pennsylvania:

Walter: "To awaken inwardly means to return to an easy and pleasant way of going through your day."

Mary: "Your aim is not to make things go according to what you call right, but according to your understanding, for that alone is right."

Carl: "You can have other people agree with you, or you

can have agreement from your own nature, but you can't have both."

Lucille: "To have beneficial values in your life it is first necessary to uncover and abandon false values."

Ralph: "Whatever you can do for yourself you can do right now, for you are not chained by time."

Anyone can return to his originally pure nature, just as we climb a mountain to a stream's pure source.

IN THE ROSE GARDEN

A teacher of ancient China was talented at finding spiritual lessons in nature. One time he and some friends were seated in a rose garden. From time to time, various birds crossed before them, flying from one side of the garden to the other.

"Your thoughts should fly like those birds," the lesson began. "They should be permitted to rise, fly past your mental vision, then disappear on the other side. Do you know the cause of personal grief? It is a man's unwise attempt to cling to a thought as if it were his personal possession. For example, many unhappy people cling desperately to thrilling thoughts. Observe each thought, then let it fly away. In this mental freedom is spontaneous happiness."

Suffering exists only when the mind runs along in mechanical thought, so to end anguish, learn how to replace habitual thought with consciousness.

THE AUTHORITY

A man who considered himself an authority on travel once found himself hiking through a desolate land. On the first evening he slept within inches of a deep pit which he did not see in the darkness. The next night he slept alongside a dozing lion which he mistook for a log. On the third night he slept within a few yards of a camp of bandits, but in the darkness they did not see each other.

Finishing his trip, the fortunate traveler told everyone, "For safety's sake, travel as I advise."

Listen to the counsel of your own original nature, not to those who do not know but imagine they do.

GLENN'S STORY

Glenn came to class with a definite idea in his mind. "I sense the practical power of these ideas," he said. "May I give an example?"

Encouraged by the nods from others, Glenn began, "A story will illustrate my point. A man once owned a very expensive horse. It cost him considerable money and time to feed and attend. But strangely, the horse returned no practical services. It was no good to ride and it refused to pull a wagon. Finally coming to his senses, the man turned the horse loose in the hills.

"This shows how man lives from artificial personality," said Glenn. "The false sense of self is utterly worthless. It costs happiness. Most men never investigate themselves and so remain unaware of their false personality. They pay the price. We are here to stop paying."

An excellent method for ceasing to pay the price of artificiality is to honestly suspect the presence of artificiality.

YOUR REAL NATURE

Said a student to his teacher, "I wish to speak from myself, not from unconscious imitation of what others have told me. How is this achieved?"

"By understanding that you never talk from yourself when you talk from memory. You are no more your memory than you are the book from which you took some facts. Memory is the past, the old, the chained. Your real nature is the present, the new, the free."

The student nodded and said, "I understand."

"Ah!" exclaimed the teacher. "Now you are talking from yourself!"

Your true nature does not depend upon memory for psychological security; therefore it performs freely and perfectly in the present moment.

THE SUPREME LAW

There was once a citizen in a country which had ten million laws. The laws were so confusing and contradictory they kept the citizen afraid and guilty all day long. He asked dozens of publicly-prominent people if it were possible to be free of his feelings of oppression. However, he observed that his advisors were just as afraid and guilty as he was.

His search finally brought him to a man who affirmed, "There exists a supreme law. Obey it and man-made laws will not trouble you. Every man is given this law at birth, but he forgets it. Look for this supreme law at home."

Searching through an old trunk in the cellar, the citizen found the supreme law. It read: *Obey the law of your own original nature.*

All feelings of oppression can be repealed by reuniting yourself with the supreme law of your true nature.

LESSONS FOR RECOVERING A NATURAL LIFE

1. Dare to step out of the known and the familiar to journey toward the unlimited world.

2. Remember that your aim is to recover your original and your untroubled nature.

3. The abandonment of a wrong position recovers the energy needed for self-transformation.

4. Realize that anxious thoughts have no real power to interfere with the natural flow of your day.

5. The aim of society is to keep everyone imprisoned, so make it your aim to refuse psychological imprisonment.

6. Let your true nature, not your conditioned self, judge whether a teaching is true or not, for it is always right.

7. Life is delightfully simple to whoever lives according to natural laws.

8. Natural happiness is recovered just as swiftly as we toss out wrong and hardened thoughts about life.

9. Artificiality demands a high price, but when living from natural principles we do not pay it.

10. You are now uniting yourself with natural law, which means you are now on your way back home.

Chapter 8

FREEDOM FROM FEAR AND NERVOUS TENSION

TUNNELS

An astronomer drove daily to the observatory located on top of a mountain. The upward road passed through a series of tunnels. The astronomer was a spiritual scientist as well as an observer of stars. One morning while on his upward drive he reflected, "This road is like the inward journey. There are dark tunnels along the way, but entering them and passing through is the certain way to reach the desired destination. There are no obstacles in the tunnel. The only barrier is our own timidity."

The astronomer continued, "What tunnel can I enter and pass through today? I know. One part of me still believes that riches and fame can make me less afraid. But a scared human being who becomes rich and famous will still be a scared human being. I will work on that idea."

The man who makes it to the top is the one who plunges through all inward tunnels, never attributing any power to them.

VILLAGE IN VENEZUELA

A village in the highlands of Venezuela was visited by a

team of engineers. Their work was to lay a water pipe from a lake to the village. While a crowd of curious children watched, a pump was installed to carry the water over a hill which stood between the lake and the village.

One afternoon, as the children watched in wonderment water poured out of the pipe at the village. One of the awed boys shyly confessed to an engineer, "I could not understand how water could run uphill."

The engineer asked, "Why didn't you ask?"

The boy answered, "I was afraid there was no answer."

Get rid of any unconscious fear that the answers to life may not exist—for they do exist.

THE CAUSE OF INSECURITY

Fred and Patricia, who came to class together, said they had the same question: "What is the real cause of mental insecurity?"

"The basic cause is a man's imaginations about who he is. For instance, he falsely thinks he is a controller, a giver, a winner. As long as exterior events seem to confirm these illusory identities he feels secure and sunny. But when they don't—and they often don't—he feels lost and desperate. You must end all self-pictures, after which you no longer fight exterior events, but blend with them. This is the way of sanity and liberty. An actor who quits the stage never worries over performances."

Life-correction consists of thinking correctly toward ourselves, after which we think wisely toward everything else.

THE FOOLISH MAN'S FUTURE

A foolish man asked a wise man, "Can you forecast my future?"

"Yes," replied the wise man, "I can tell your psychological future. You will be nervous, irritable and jealous."

"How can I avoid these painful states?"

"For one thing, give up your greedy goals."

"I wish you would not call them greedy goals," said the foolish man with resentment. "I call them worthwhile ambitions."

"That is your problem. You use words like paint to make evil look like good."

"Well," said the foolish man as he stood up to leave, "all this is very interesting. Maybe we can talk again."

"No," said the wise man. "You will never be back. Both of us know that."

Every man has a psychological future which he can make right with sincere intentions in today.

THE SHADOWS AHEAD

Three friends were passing through a strange land at night. Just ahead they saw some moving shadows which seemed to menace them.

"We had better run away," whispered one.

"No, it is best to rush forward and fight them," stated another.

Advised the third man, "Let's sit quietly here until we understand what they are."

So that is what they did. At dawn, the shadows which seemed so menacing turned out to be broad branches of a tree.

The inaction of a quiet mind is the only action leading to perception of things as they are.

A REAL SOURCE OF HELP

A group of disciples left the lecture hall after a particularly powerful message from their teacher. A young student commented, "It is almost frightening the way the master exposes our pretenses. Part of me wants to run away and hide." Other pupils nodded in agreement.

Said an advanced student with a smile, "Truly you are beginners on the path. Be neither frightened nor angry to-

ward a teacher who sees through you, for he is the only kind
of person who can really help you."

*Careful attention to our truth-lessons makes them ap-
pear less and less like hawks and look more and more like
the doves that they are.*

THE UNIFORMS

There was once a man who owned dozens of uniforms
and costumes. He wore the uniform which seemed best for
the occasion. For example, when wanting to appear wise
he wore a judge's robe, while at a party he dressed like a
clown. Playing his uniformed roles seemed to provide security, for he needed only to glance at his costume to know
who he was.

But over the years he noticed something. While removing one uniform and putting on another he felt terrified, for
in that minute he did not know who he was.

The man finally consulted a sage who told him, "You
have noticed something quite valuable. Get rid of your uniforms and dress normally. Have no fear in doing this, for
you will then know who you really are."

*Social uniforms consist of self-dramatizing thoughts, so
by dropping them we rest in our own normality.*

THE BULL IN THE FIELD

A man and his son were crossing a field when a vicious
bull appeared before them, half-hidden by some bushes.
The terrified boy started to run away, but his father calmly
called him back. "See," said the father with a gesture, "the
bull is chained. You were safe all along."

As they walked on, the father said, "Fear is a terrible
emotion, which you need not suffer from. Learn to see a
situation as *it* is, not as *you* are."

*When you are truly transformed, so is your world, and
that world contains no fear.*

CORRECTED MISTAKES

Members of a class in Ohio told of self-harming attitudes they had corrected:

Gerald: "There was no way for truth to get through to me until I realized at last that I was a prisoner who refused his own liberty."

Elizabeth: "Do not allow the behavior of other people to be your model, or you will suffer from what they suffer."

David: "Not realizing that it was really possible to know, I used to content myself with pretending to know."

Dorothy: "A person who has taken his own responsibilities will never wrongly bear the responsibilities belonging to others."

Stephen: "I saw that true victory is not over people and events, but over my own wrong and unconscious ideas."

Our task is to neither excuse our mistakes nor blame others for them, but to determine their causes within ourselves.

THE HERMIT

A citizen fleeing from a wicked king found refuge in a cave on the side of a mountain. There he lived for years in nervous discomfort. Not only did he fear capture, but huge boulders crashed constantly around his head.

One morning, weary of his fearful existence, he climbed cautiously to the plateau above the cave. There he met a group of happy people who told him the king had no power to reach them.

Complained the hermit, "Why didn't you tell me about this before?"

Someone answered, "You never asked."

People live in a world of fear because they do not question the necessity for doing so.

THE ANGRY MAN

There was once a man who had been treated roughly by

life. He wrongly used it as an excuse for hostile behavior. As he daily showed his anger to others, he discovered that people were easily shaken by his hostility. So he enjoyed the power his animosity seemed to supply. He felt important and individualistic.

One day he met a stranger, and, as usual, showed anger. But the stranger reacted in a different way than the others. His eyes seemed to see past the anger and into the man himself. The stranger then said in a calm voice, "There is no need to be afraid."

The hostile man began to think about that.

Fear goes with anger, and anger goes with fear, but there is no need for either of them.

UNEXPECTED EVENTS

Asked a student in class, "Is it possible to live without fear of the unknown and the unexpected?"

"Yes."

"How?"

"Give up the belief that you possess a separate self which is apart from the Whole. Then, in this self-unity you are also in unity with every event in your day. In this total union there can be no battling opposites and therefore no fear."

"I will try to understand."

"Good. The understanding of Oneness is everything."

Insight into Oneness ends a thousand fears and tensions.

WHAT THE MAN FEARED

At a gathering of friends, one man was boasting of his fearlessness. With great pride he described his daring adventures in dense jungles and on stormy seas. He concluded, "I even give lectures in which I tell others how to be unafraid."

Several of his friends gently suggested there might be more vanity than veracity in his assertions.

"Nonsense!" he exploded. "Tell me one thing I fear."

"You fear we will see how afraid you are."

To pretend to not be afraid of something prevents the healing in which we are really not afraid.

WHY ANXIETY CONTINUES

Harvey, an insurance agent, asked, "Why does anxiety continue in spite of all attempts to end it?"

"Think of the last time you searched for a lost article. Did you notice something? Everything was fine as long as you still had places to look. But as you began to run out of likely places, anxiety arose. Man is like that. Fearing coming to an end of himself, he pretends he still has legitimate places to look. He must come to the end of his self-deceiving search. What he has lost can be found, but not as long as he insists upon looking in the wrong places."

Look inward, for the healing is in the same place as the hurt.

THE AUTHORITATIVE ATTENDANT

A man was visiting a sick friend in a hospital. While they were conversing, an attendant entered. By his self-important manner, the attendant revealed his love for his authority over the patients. When the attendant approached the sick friend, the visitor stepped away, found a vacant bed and relaxed upon it.

The attendant then approached the visitor, eyed him quizzically for a moment, and thrust out a bottle of medicine.

"I am sorry," apologized the visitor, "but I am not sick."

Do not be intimidated by those who love their authority in human affairs, for your inner spirit possesses true authority.

HOW SUFFERING ENDED

There was once a man who insisted he knew what he

was talking about. Consequently, he talked only with those who talked as he talked and avoided those who talked differently. Those who agreed with him were called friends, while those who disagreed were called enemies.

But the man lived in terrible tension. He could never find enough friends and was always harassed by enemies. Still, he received an odd enjoyment from his nervous agitation.

One day his supposed friends deserted him. Although suffering terribly, he noticed something peculiar. By losing his friends he also lost his enemies. From that day on he sensed how his suffering could end. And when he finally understood, his suffering did end.

Both friends and enemies exist as ideas in a divided mind, so by rising above these ideas a man becomes unified, and therefore truly friendly.

THE PRINCES AND THE LION

A king of ancient Babylon had two young sons. One day the king's soldiers brought a caged lion to the palace for all to see. The king took the hands of the boys and led them to the lion. The lion suddenly roared, which so frightened one of the princes that he ran away.

That evening, the prince who had remained with the lion told his brother all about the strange creature. The frightened boy was impressed with his brother's knowledge, and said so. "It was easy," came the reply. "I just stood there and studied."

The person who eventually understands what life is all about is the person who does not run away.

THE STRANGE MAGICIANS

A girl ran home to tell her father about a marvelous magician she had seen. Excitedly, she described how the magician had made doves and flowers appear out of the air.

Her father responded, "You know, other people also perform strange acts of magic. I know a man who makes enemies appear out of nowhere. Also, a woman down the street pulls problems out of empty space. In reality, neither enemies nor problems exist except in their confused minds."

Part of the girl's mind heard and recorded her father's unexpected words. Years later she understood the lesson and felt grateful.

The psychic magician is one who no longer creates his own problems and griefs.

THE LIGHT OF SELF-HONESTY

Keith stated, "All of us sense the power of self-honesty. How can we make it work for us?"

"When a man takes an unpleasant fact about himself as a fact, and not as a hurtful criticism, it ceases to be a fact. This is mental magic. Suppose a deceitful man is told that he is deceitful. He wrongly takes it as a criticism but not as a fact. By refusing to face the fact the self-punishment of deceit must continue, such as the punishment of nervousness. But when honestly taking it as a fact he admits self-light. This light then reveals that deceit *is* self-punishing. Seeing this, deceit vanishes of itself, for self-punishment never continues when seen as self-punishment. Honesty is light. Light cancels darkness."

People who say they want help and encouragement need look nowhere else but toward their own self-honesty.

THE CREEPER

A teacher's assistant was guiding a group of beginners to the esoteric school. While passing through some shadowy woods the assistant said, "Watch out for the Creeper. The Creeper is an animal living in these woods. It may suddenly appear in front of you."

The beginners whispered worriedly among themselves

for a moment. One of them finally asked the assistant, "If there is danger from the Creeper, why did you bring us this way?"

The assistant reached behind a nearby bush and held up a small and innocent-eyed rabbit. "Creeper," he said, "is the local name for this breed of rabbit. You now have your first lesson. You were afraid of a mere word, which prevented you from understanding the fact."

Understanding exists on a higher level than both words and the associations aroused by words.

GUILT AND DESPERATION

There was once a man who suffered daily from guilt and desperation. A wise friend asked him, "Would you like to know how to get rid of guilt?"

The sufferer instantly snapped, "I already know."

The friend persisted, "Would you like me to tell you how to banish desperation?"

The man replied with pride, "I already know."

"But if you already know, how come you still suffer from guilt and desperation? Would you like to know how to end your self-punishing confusion?"

The suffering man stated, "I already know."

Just as darkness is merely the absence of light, fearful resistance to truth is simply the absence of understanding.

THE CANDLE

There was once a young candle which did not understand his purpose in being a candle. He thought his only need was to illuminate himself, so he hugged his flame as tightly as he could. As a result of this his light did not reach the other parts of the room, which made him afraid of the shadowy shapes out there.

Later, growing tired of being afraid, he loosened his light to let it illumine the whole room. Then the shadowy shapes disappeared and he was no longer afraid.

Fear arises from the false belief in a separate self, so fear departs with the understanding of Oneness.

HOW TO END WORRY

When attending her first class, Susan had mentioned her specific worries, including worry over money and her human relations. At a later session she asked, "How can we understand and end worry?"

"What would the mind do if it had nothing to worry about? The very question frightens a mind which operates wrongly. Above all it fears coming to the end of itself. If it has nothing to worry about it immediately seizes something. Why all this foolish mental agitation? Because a man's supposed identity, such as being successful, acts upon the stage of thought. He fears the end of thought because he wrongly believes it means the end of himself. But it will only end the false self with all its anguish. Worry is false action, like a man who jumps up and down to convince himself he is traveling somewhere."

Useless thought can come to an end, but we must experiment with this until the miracle of consciousness appears.

THE SUBSTITUTE

A man returned home from a meeting of his club. His wife asked, "Did the speaker give an interesting talk?"

"I don't know," her husband replied.

"But you were there."

"Yes, but the scheduled speaker failed to appear. I was chosen as the substitute speaker."

"Well, did *you* give an interesting talk?"

"I don't know. I was so nervous I wasn't listening."

Nothing need distract us from hearing the voice of our own essence.

HOWLING WOLVES

A pioneer in an unsettled wilderness was visited by a

friend. As they sat down to dinner, some wolves howled fiercely near the cabin's door. The pioneer proceeded calmly with dinner, but the visitor jumped nervously. "You are not alarmed?" he asked.

The pioneer replied, "They often howl near the door. At first I was scared of them. But I decided to study the nature of wolves, and I learned many things. It was my own wrong reaction to them which caused fear, for they have no real power to harm me. Nowadays their howls stop at my ears; they no longer penetrate inwardly to cause disturbance. You can say I am no longer at home to them. They howl in vain. How can they hurt anyone who is no longer at home to them?"

You can learn to not be at home to wolves of worry or of loneliness or any other kinds of wolves.

A SUMMARY OF IDEAS FOR ENDING FEAR

1. Fear may have a terrifying appearance, but has no power whatever to whoever lives from his cosmic mind.

2. If you state that the answers to life exist, you make a perfectly accurate statement.

3. The secret of secrets is to stop setting negative causes into motion, for that makes every new moment a free moment.

4. Simply remember that fear and nervousness cannot exist in a mind which sees things as they are.

5. Oneness with yourself is the same as oneness with the universe, and that universe does not include fear.

6. Constantly question the necessity of anxiety, and you will eventually hear the answer that it is completely unnecessary.

7. Apprehension will not remain with the man or woman who sees through its bluff.

8. Man is fearfully separated from himself by illusion only, so when the illusion is cured, so is the man.

9. Realize that self-honesty is a necessity, an inspiration, and a power for self-transcendence.

10. The tyranny of fear comes to an end by uncovering the lamp of your own mind.

Chapter 9

STRANGE FACTS ABOUT MAN AND HIS WAYS

THE GROUP MEETING

Several people once met in group therapy with the stated purpose of clearing confusion from their lives.

One of them talked so much that the others glared at him in contempt. Another one who considered himself an authority felt hurt when everyone ignored him. Another person sat quietly and observed a member of the opposite sex across the room. A fourth person sat there in depression and wondered why he had come in the first place.

At the end of the meeting, everyone said what a helpful evening it had been. But they never met again.

Only right aims and intentions can illuminate a room where people gather for self-help.

THE REFORMER

A citizen said to a famous reformer, "Please explain. You condemn society for violence, yet your protests are equally violent."

"There is a big difference," said the reformer.

"You demand that other people respect you, but you never speak of your need to respect them."

"There is a big difference."

"You criticize other groups for putting on pressure, yet the entire purpose of your group is to apply pressure."

"There is a big difference."

"What is the big difference?"

"How stupid you are. We are good, while others are evil."

A man can be empowered by delusion or by self-knowledge, but only self-insight changes anything.

A STRANGE FACT ABOUT SUFFERING

A teacher of esotericism entered the classroom and wrote five sentences on the blackboard:

Stop loving your suffering.

Stop enjoying your persecution.

Stop adoring your anxiety.

Stop cherishing your resentment.

Stop glorifying your failure.

"You may think," the teacher told his pupils, "that people want to end their suffering and persecution. In fact, they fight like tigers to keep them. Why? Because suffering provides an excuse for egotism. The sufferer is able to remain the center of both his own attention and the attention of others. If you want spiritual rebirth, give up your love for such foolishness."

A sincere willingness to abandon the false pleasure of suffering will reveal the supremacy of peace.

ACTRESS ANN

"It is incredible," said Ann in group discussion, "but I now see why self-observation is so vital. Quiet self-viewing is the beginning of self-change, a change toward health and happiness."

Asked Jerry, "What, exactly, did you observe in yourself?"

"Something startling," said Ann. "I saw how I secretly resented people who expected me to behave in a certain way toward them. I was like an actress given a difficult role she really did not want to play. I now see how fearful I was of the disapproval of my audience. You know, I would never have believed this about myself unless I had seen it for myself."

"None of us believe it at the start," added Isabel, "but thank heaven we are waking up."

A refusal to remain in psychic sleep is a power in itself for self-awakening.

ADRIFT AT SEA

When their ship sank in a storm, six men and women found themselves at sea in a small boat. On the first day they felt confident, but later turned gloomy when no sign of rescue appeared.

"I think," said one of the men on the third day, "we should promise heaven to lead more noble lives in exchange for rescue." All agreed. Just as they were about to raise their hands in a vow, someone shouted, "Wait! Not so fast! I see land!"

No person ever changes his nature until he deeply sees the absolute folly of living as he does.

THE BOX OF CHOCOLATES

As class ended, a teacher set a book of wisdom and a large box of chocolates next to each other on a table. "Take whichever you prefer," invited the teacher.

All the students but one crowded around the book of wisdom. They commented seriously upon the ideas in the book.

The other student opened the box of chocolates and helped himself. Noticing the doubtful gaze of the other students he stated, "I see just as much wisdom in the chocolates as in the book. I observed my own attraction to the candy. I watched my hand reach out to it. I was aware of its pleasurable taste. You have no idea how much this candy taught me about myself. Also," the student added with a smile, "I was conscious that most of you really preferred the chocolates."

Everyone else also smiled, including the teacher.

A school of wisdom is wherever a self-working person happens to be, whether at home, in an office, or anywhere else.

TRADER TRAVIS

A tourist was strolling down a quiet street in an unfamiliar town when he saw a shop sign: *TRADER TRAVIS.* Curious, he entered to ask, "What products do you trade?"

"Oh, many things," replied Trader Travis. "Give me your Anxiety and I will give you Poise. Give me Gullibility and you can have Insight."

"Astounding!" exclaimed the tourist. "How busy you must be!"

Trader Travis shook his head. "Not at all. You see, many people do not value my products. Others cannot believe that items such as Conscience and Compassion can actually be found, while still others believe they already have them. But once in awhile I do get a customer. How about you?"

Welcome the healing facts as you would want the healing facts to welcome you.

THE DIVIDED VILLAGE

There was once a village in which everyone lived in harmony. One day the people went out to pick the berries which grew in abundance in surrounding fields. Those who picked purple berries stained their clothes with that color. Those gathering orange berries were stained with orange color. When the people looked at the stains an odd thing happened. Some immediately called themselves the *Purple People*, while the others labeled themselves the *Orange*

People. From that day on the village was divided into two hostile groups who fought night and day.

A wise man who was passing through the village was asked, "Is it possible for the people to stop fighting?"

"Yes," he said, "if they ever get over the childish vanity of calling themselves by special names."

Every human problem and heartache can be cured by seeing through society's labels.

PSYCHIC HYPNOSIS

In a class in Minnesota the teacher said, "Remember, you are constantly given facts which you do not accept presently, which have no meaning to you. For instance, if I say you are now seated before me in a state of psychic hypnosis, you do not understand what this means. Not understanding, you either reject it or think it applies to the person next to you. But the plain fact remains that you are now listening to me while immersed in spiritual and psychological hypnosis, which you do not realize."

"How can realization come?" asked Douglas.

"Listen without resistance; let facts have their way, not just now, but tomorrow and next week and next month and next year."

When you know how to be free of mental conditioning you also know how to be free of psychic hypnosis.

THE TIGER SHOES

There was once a country with a proud tradition. As a symbol of strength its citizens wore shoes which displayed a picture of a tiger. However, the land was rough and rocky, so the shoes wore out quickly, causing discomfort.

But there was one shoemaker who made sturdy and durable shoes, always comfortable to whoever wore them. When glancing at the shoes, people asked him, "Where is the picture of the tiger?" He replied patiently, "I have no pictures. I just make strong shoes."

"You have no sense of what is right," accused most people, as they limped away in pain.

Man conceals his weaknesses under theatrical symbols, then wonders why he limps through life.

THE GREAT DIFFERENCE

A man visited his friend at an esoteric school. The visitor was eager to meet the teacher, for he had heard that he was a man of extraordinary spiritual attainments. But after seeing the teacher, the visitor spoke with disappointment to his friend, "I see nothing unusual about him."

"Of course you don't. It is spiritual law that no man can see above his own level. His supremacy exists, but not to you. A rabbit knows nothing about a star."

"I still don't see how he is different. He walks and talks much like anyone else."

"When he walks and talks, do you know the great difference between you and him?"

"What?"

"You do them mechanically. He does them *consciously.*"

For the next few hours, try to see the difference between mechanical behavior and conscious action.

PSYCHIC POWERS

A man who had found a genuine teacher was asked how he had succeeded. "I knew only one thing," explained the man, "but I knew it for sure. I knew that a true teacher never bluffs. Bluffing is a stupid man's attempt to appear wise. Sooner or later, all teachers are asked about psychic powers. A false teacher bluffs out his answer. He promises supernatural rewards to his followers, or boasts about miracles he has seen, or hints that he himself possesses occult powers."

"And how did the authentic teacher reply?"

"He told us to give up our childish attraction to psychic powers and to try for just one hour to not think a destructive thought."

There is something different about the answers of an authentic teacher, which is detected by people having something different in themselves.

WHAT A FREE MAN IS LIKE

A teacher in Australia asked his class of advanced students, "What is a free man like?" The replies came:

Ruth: "Since he understands why things happen as they do, he can guide others to safety."

Merle: "He does not live from borrowed opinions, as do most men, but lives from his own pure essence."

Dean: "An expert in human nature, he perceives dozens of facts about a man that the man himself never even suspects."

Maxine: "He knows that the best things in life are invisible."

Hugh: "Having no psychological attachment to his listeners, he has something truly good for them."

Shirley: "Unlike most men, he really sees that a simple goodness is right after all."

Our aim is to know what a free man is like by personal experience.

THE BOTTLE OF WATER

Two men were digging potatoes on a hot day. Pausing for a drink, they discovered they had only one small bottle of water between them. "We will divide it half and half," said the first man, to which the second man agreed.

The first man put the bottle to his lips and quickly drank all of the water. His companion protested loudly. The first man lowered the bottle, shook his head slowly and said in a very serious tone, "You must try to understand. I know how it appears to you, but my behavior was both logical and necessary. You see, my half of the water was on the bottom."

Greed cunningly attempts to justify itself.

THE PECULIAR RAINFALL

A certain country had a peculiar kind of rainfall. On some days it rained pure water which gave health and refreshment to the citizens. But on other days the rain was impure, causing illness and discomfort.

Most citizens of the land were unaware of the difference in the two kinds of rain. Also, they had no interest in analyzing the nature of rainfall. Consequently, illness was common in the country.

But one of the citizens did not like being sick. So studying the rainfall, he soon saw the difference in the two kinds. Able to distinguish between pure and impure water, he set out his water barrel only when the rainfall was healthy.

One of our early tasks is to distinguish between healthy facts and popular illusions.

A FAMILIAR PUZZLE

During the question and answer period of a class the teacher was asked, "We would like an explanation of a familiar puzzle. Human beings can study the virtuous teachings of religion and philosophy for many years and yet show little personal evidence of the virtues they talk about. Why?"

"Because they mistake the method of transportation for the destination. It is as if someone climbs into his car in New York and then announces he has reached his home in Boston. To reach home we must go beyond intellectual knowledge to an abandonment of the false self."

The spiritual journey consists of traveling beyond vanity-feeding thoughts about personal goodness to the cosmic goodness of the ego-free man.

THE DESPERATE WOMAN

A desperate woman asked a teacher, "How can I change my life?" He told her, "Make a personal effort to abandon your old ways."

Not caring for personal effort, the woman repeated to another teacher, "How can I change my life?" She heard, "Think new thoughts."

But preferring her habitual thoughts, she looked around for another advisor. Meeting a man with a public reputation for knowing all the answers, she asked the usual question, "How can I change my life?"

Smiling, he assured her, "You need do nothing but put yourself into our capable hands. We will take care of everything."

"Thank heaven!" exclaimed the woman. "I have found a compassionate teacher at last. And a miracle-worker! He will show me how to change my life without changing my life!"

There is always medicine for earnest people, but none for the foolish, for they cannot distinguish between medicine and syrup.

THE CROW AND THE HAWK

A crow was standing in the sun in a position which made his shadow much larger than the crow himself. Thinking that the shadow represented his true size, the crow became foolish and arrogant. Sighting a nearby hawk, the crow flew toward it, intending to taunt the larger bird. The hawk suddenly drew himself up in a show of strength, which shocked the crow out of his arrogance.

The hawk, who had observed the crow with his shadow, advised, "Take another look at yourself. You are not that shadow."

Because man lives from self-flattering imaginations about himself, he pays the shocking price.

RICH AND FAMOUS

During a lecture a teacher suddenly asked his students, "Why do you want to climb a coconut tree?"

One student timidly answered for the puzzled class,

"But sir, we do not want to climb a coconut tree. There is no reason for it."

"No reason for it?" replied the teacher. "I see. You know, if you ask a man why he wants to become rich and famous he will answer you, but will be mouthing mere words. He will not really know why, *for there is no why*. There is no reason on earth to become rich and famous. Your own cosmic completeness will make this clear."

Find yourself, after which you will not wearily waste yourself in trying to find useless objects.

THE BATTLERS

A man who lived on a mountain looked down at a man who lived in the valley below. "Obviously," said the mountain man, "I was meant to rule the valley man."

The valley man looked up and reflected, "Apparently, I was meant to serve the mountain man."

So agreeing upon that arrangement, all went well between them for awhile. But one day, by accident, the valley man found himself on the mountain. It changed him. Insisting that he was supposed to be the ruler, he viciously threw the mountain man into the valley.

So they battled endlessly, with one on top and then the other. Between battles they signed peace treaties.

But neither ever inquired as to the cause of their misery.

Self-inquiry reveals the nature of all things, and that revelation is self-liberty.

THE FOLLOWERS

There was once a famous magician who astounded everyone by making almost any object disappear. His showmanship attracted many followers who attended every performance. One day he performed before an audience on board a ship. The ship sank in a sudden storm, but the magician and his devotees managed to make it to a lifeboat.

"Wonderful!" the people praised and applauded the magician. "But tell us, where did you hide the ship?"

Hero-worship is not far from gullibility.

THE PARROT

There was once a parrot who trained himself to speak excellently. This enabled him to teach other parrots to speak, for which he was honored and applauded. But he had a secret sorrow. He did not know how to fly. But he devised a clever method for concealing his humiliation. Using his superb command of words, he told other parrots how to fly.

His lectures on flying were a huge success. Thousands assembled each week to hear his dynamic exhortations.

And few of his hearers ever suspected that the parrot himself did not know how to fly.

A man seldom realizes that spiritual lessons apply to him personally, thus making him an eager reformer of other people.

IN THE BAKERY

There was once a baker who diligently sought and finally found the secrets of life. He wrote his discoveries in a book and placed the volume on a counter in his bakery. Calling in several unhappy friends he announced, "In this book are the answers you seek." One by one the men spoke up:

"What a delicious-looking chocolate cake!"

"How much are those coconut cookies?"

"What an aroma from that fresh bread!"

"I'll take two of your great apple pies."

Only one man picked up and studied the book.

Man is so distracted by habitual sights and desires he cannot grasp the truth even when it sets plainly before him.

WHAT AN AWAKENED MAN SEES

Ronald asked, "What does an awakened man see that other people do not perceive?"

"He is like an observer standing on a hilltop, watching the frantic chasings of men and women on the prairie below. Among other insights, he sees these hypnotized men setting traps for each other. The traps are always attractively decorated, to make them appear beneficial. The awakened man sees clearly all the resulting heartache. You may ask why he does not shout down to them a warning of what they do to each other. He does, but here we meet one of the peculiar features of the tragedy. *Man is unable to hear.* He is spiritually deaf.

"But those who listen will hear. These people neither set traps nor fall into them."

Self-awakening enables you to see the human scene as it is, not as it appears to be, which frees you of its chaos.

OUTSTANDING PRINCIPLES IN REVIEW

1. Check and correct your aims every day to make sure they lead toward higher goals.

2. Astonishingly, if you will have absolutely nothing to do with suffering, suffering will have nothing to do with you.

3. Let refusal be your ready power, such as refusing to be guided by anything but your own enlightened mind.

4. Your own mind is a school of true knowledge which you can attend every moment of the day.

5. Travel beyond mere words, beyond labels, beyond society's dramatic but empty performances.

6. Today, think what it means to walk consciously, to speak with self-awareness, to be one with yourself at all times.

7. Never accept a way of life as being right simply because it is publicly popular or rewarding, but build your own way from yourself.

8. True goodness consists of union with cosmic goodness, which is not mysterious, but perfectly plain to sincere seekers.

9. Cosmic completeness releases you from dozens of tiring tasks you really do not want to do.

10. Whoever has cleared himself of inner chaos remains untouched by the chaos of a hysterical society.

Chapter 10

HOW TO TURN EMOTIONS
INTO HEALING POWERS

THE MAN WITHOUT A CARE

A motorist was driving through farming country when he saw a man working alongside the road. When the motorist stopped to ask for directions, they fell into conversation. The motorist observed the great amount of work to be done, including irrigation and fence-mending.

"With all the necessary work out there," remarked the motorist with a sweeping gesture, "your mind must be in endless turmoil."

"No," replied the other man. "I don't have a care in the world."

"But the farm requires so many difficult decisions."

"Yes, but I don't own it."

An individual without a sense of personal ownership toward life is carefree, with no difficult decisions to make.

THE ROCK

While conducting a class in a shady grove a teacher said, "I want you to see the burden of having an angry mind. Also, I want you to see that the hiding of anger is not the same as the absence of anger." The teacher then in-

structed a student to pick up a heavy rock and set it down
again. The student groaningly did so, after which the teacher next instructed, "Place your coat over it." The student
obeyed.

"Now tell me," the teacher asked the class, "is that
covered rock just as heavy as it was before?"

*The burden of any kind of negative emotion is lifted by
exposing and understanding it.*

CONCEALED WEAPONS

A citizen of a violent nation decided to emigrate to another country. When reaching the border of the new nation
the guards asked, "Do you have any concealed weapons?"
Admitting he had, the guards turned back his several attempts to cross.

On one more attempt a guard asked, "Why carry concealed weapons?" The man explained their necessity in
his violent nation.

The guard explained, "You misunderstand. This is a
peaceful land. There is no need for weapons of any kind."

In relief, the emigrant abandoned his concealed weapons and entered the new nation.

*When dwelling within cosmic consciousness, there is no
need for concealed weapons, such as suppressed resent-
ments.*

THE SHIVERING MAN

It was the month of August, but instead of the usual
heat, the day was chilly. A foolish man walked down the
street, coatless and shivering. An approaching friend remarked, "You look cold."

"Impossible!" declared the shivering man. "This is
August."

"Never mind what the calendar says," advised his
friend. "What does your body say?"

*An honest appraisal of how we really feel is necessary
if we wish to change and feel right.*

EXHAUSTED DONALD

Donald's business affairs took him to different parts of the United States. Whenever he could find a class in authentic esotericism, he paid it a visit. In a class in Florida, Donald confessed, "I am tired, but the cause of my exhaustion is not clear to me."

"And you are interested in knowing what it is?"

"Very much interested."

"You are tired of looking after yourself."

After a short pause, Donald nodded in understanding. "Yes, that's it. Of course. You cleared it up in a flash. What must I do?"

"See that you are not the self you think you are. You are not your personal dreams and habits and ambitions. You are part of the Whole."

Nothing is more exhausting than to haul around a fictitious sense of self, and nothing is more relieving than to drop it.

THE STORM

A group of friends rented a mountain cabin for a few days. When an unexpected storm kept them indoors, the first few hours were spent in pleasant conversation. But one man suddenly revealed a deep bitterness by complaining of past mistreatment by people. Surprised by his outburst, the others said little.

Next morning, the complainer asked someone who had just stepped out the door, "Is it still storming?"

"Not out here."

It is the inner storm which needs attention and correction.

FIGHTING AND FUSSING

There was once a Nobody who wanted to become a

Somebody. So he said to himself, "Like everyone else who wants to become a Somebody, I will start fighting and fussing."

That is what he did. Fighting and fussing became his way of life. He made some strange discoveries. The very fighting and fussing made him feel like Somebody, even though unrecognized as such by others. Also, when becoming Somebody in a small town he felt the painfully compulsive urge to become Somebody in a large city.

One day he grew weary of the miserable excitement of fighting and fussing, so he decided to be a Nobody again. It was difficult at first, for excitement had become a fixed habit. But he finally saw that Nobody and Somebody were mere words which deluded human beings took as realities. Then, all was well with him.

Man's hypnotic love for emotional agitation, in preference to truth, explains every human tragedy.

THE RIGHT FEELING

A tailor was visited regularly by salesmen who showed him a wide variety of fabrics. While displaying sample material, the salesmen called attention to the attractive patterns and bright colors. The tailor always listened quietly to the salesmen, then requested them to set all the material on a table. Closing his eyes, the tailor ran his fingers over each sample. After feeling a fabric he remarked, "This feels right," or, "This one does not feel right."

The tailor purchased or declined to purchase according to the feeling he received from a fabric. He explained, "Clothing is very intimate, very close to an individual. It is good for him to look right, but essential that he feels right."

We feel right by clothing ourselves in right ideas.

THE BEAUTY OF SIMPLICITY

A stream once flowed peacefully and pleasantly down the side of a mountain. It was discovered by some men who cared nothing for its beauty. In order to dig a mine the men forced the stream out of its natural course. For the next few years the stream flowed between some rocky hills. Its flow was often interrupted and blocked by falling rocks. The stream lost its natural beauty and simplicity.

But one day the mine was abandoned and the men went away. With natural movement the stream went back to its original course. No longer in unnatural surroundings, it flowed peacefully and pleasantly once more.

Be reunited with the natural and simple flow of your original nature.

THE END OF CONFUSION

A class in Dallas presented these solutions for banishing emotional confusion:

Leslie: "There is no personal inferiority or superiority except in wrong emotional reactions, which clear thinking can correct."

Edwin: "Every person is his own broadcasting station, sending out messages of harmony or of discord."

Nancy: "Deal wisely and firmly with adverse forces and you will be unafraid of them, for they attack only when detecting weakness."

Annette: "A healing lesson appears frightening at first only because we fail to understand it."

Fred: "It may be a man's way to quarrel and to agonize, but it is not the way of Higher Reality."

When rightly channeled, emotions become a form of energy for healing.

THE MAN WHO RAN

A man was strolling through the woods when he saw smoke rising from the trees. His emotions leaped, for he feared a disastrous forest fire. While racing frantically about and shouting an alarm, he fell several times, hurting himself somewhat.

There was no need for frantic running. There was no forest fire. The smoke arose from a perfectly safe campground. But this he did not see because his nervous emotions blocked natural reasoning.

If our view of life is wrong, wrong actions follow, causing unnecessary self-injury.

THE BARKING DOG

A traveler in Tibet was guiding his horse along a narrow mountain trail. At various places the path grew vague and divided. This aroused frustration, for he wanted to end the hazardous journey as soon as possible.

When approaching some bushes, a large dog leaped out, barking furiously and blocking the trail. Reluctantly halting, the annoyed traveler considered ways to get rid of this unexpected enemy.

Then a man appeared who said, "He is not trying to block your way, but to show you the way. A dangerous bend is just ahead. Keep to the right and you will be safe."

Frustration of desire seems to be an enemy only because we fail to grasp its deeper message of safe guidance.

THE VOLCANOS

A certain land was covered with hundreds of smoldering volcanos. Wishing to understand their nature, some scientists lived among the volcanos for several weeks. Part of their report read:

"The volcanos have a peculiar pattern of cause and effect. Every time a volcano erupts, its lava and smoke cross the ground to reach surrounding volcanos. The fiery touch of the erupting volcano causes the other volcanos to explode. So these volcanos have their own way of fighting among themselves, with one provoking another. However, a few volcanos are peaceful. They never attack and therefore are never attacked."

It is psychic law that a person gets what he actually gives, regardless of what he wrongly assumes he gives.

HOW TO USE SORROW

In class, Dorothy reported fine progress in straightening out her life. She explained, "My aim is to get through to myself, which calls for energetic action in knocking down the walls of my own resistance to truth." Dorothy then asked for help with a particular idea: "I am wondering about the familiar teaching about using sorrow for gain. I don't see how suffering can do any good. I dislike pain."

Dorothy and the class heard, "In itself, sorrow is indeed valueless. But you can use suffering to end suffering. If you knew the secret of turning stones into rubies, you would use those stones. Your reading and experiencing are teaching you this secret."

A wise way to use suffering is to clearly and consistently see how utterly worthless it is.

FALSE GUILT MUST GO

There was once an unhappy man who demanded of his neighbors, "You owe me a better place to live." Having a false sense of guilt, his neighbors paid his way to a better place to live. But a few days later the still unhappy man complained, "You don't show me enough respect." So his confused neighbors paid him shallow compliments, which the man eagerly devoured.

The more the unhappy man was given the more he demanded. Not knowing what else to do, his baffled neighbors usually appeased him, even while sensing it was wrong. They finally consulted a wise man who explained, "Drop your false guilt. You permit him to exploit you, so you yourselves add to his neurosis. He must save himself by becoming a conscious human being."

Realizing the truth of this, the neighbors felt much better.

It is the truth that makes you free, including the truth about the human condition.

TREE AND TREASURE

A group of men buried a treasure in a field, intending to recover it when needed. To remember its location they planted a young tree over it.

Years later, they fell into quarrels among themselves. When one man made a demand or claim, another man shouted back with his own claim. Chaos ruled.

But it was an incredibly strange dispute. They had forgotten all about the treasure. They quarreled over the tree!

Having forgotten the truth itself, man quarrels over religious words and procedures.

PAUL AND LEWIS

Two young men named Paul and Lewis lived in opposite apartments in a large city. They often exchanged greetings in the morning. Paul usually said, "I'm off to school," while Lewis replied, "I'm going to school also."

Later, Paul's college education led to wealth and fame, but they did not supply the contentment he had expected. One day Paul accidently met Lewis, and was attracted by his self-command. Curious about it, Paul asked Lewis, "What school did you attend?"

"Among other schools," replied Lewis, "I went to the school of *life*. In other words, wherever I went I went to school."

"But what did you learn?"

"I learned to never let external events tell me how to feel."

External events dictate the feelings of most human beings, but the self-unified man is no such slave.

HOW SHOCKS CAN HELP

Arthur said he and his wife had been discussing a certain idea at home. He then explained in class, "You say it is good and necessary to be shocked at our psychic sleep. Will you please review?"

"You are driving your car in heavy traffic. Your mind wanders and you make a mistake, but correct it in time to avoid an accident. First you had a shock, then you were aware that you were unaware. Now, if you simply realize you were asleep for a moment, and not blame the other driver, you wisely use that shock for future self-alertness. Your awareness of being unaware is awareness itself. All this is of great value in everyday life."

To the truly intelligent individual, shocks and humiliations are nothing more than corrective guideposts along the road.

THE TWO HORSES

A man once owned two horses which he could not tell apart. In order to distinguish one from the other he tied a rope around the neck of one horse. However, the rope fell off, so he separated the animals by a fence. But one horse leaped the fence, leaving the man as confused as before. He then asked a neighbor, "How can I tell one horse from the other?"

Studying the horses for a moment, the neighbor nodded and said, "I think I have it. Look very closely and you will see that one horse is black and the other one is white."

Man fails to see the obvious, as when he does not see the difference between what he says and the way he really feels.

THE WATERFALL

Turning a corner, a party of tourists came upon a magnificent waterfall. With loud words and wild gestures, everyone praised the sight before them.

The party's guide, who stood off to one side, was asked, "Do you still enjoy its beauty?"

"I do," sighed the guide, "until someone shouts about it."

Beauty, which originates in a quiet mind, vanishes with the appearance of mechanical emotionalism.

THE OPEN SEA

There was once a boat which was careful to remain within the quiet waters of the harbor. When finding itself drifting toward the open sea it quickly dropped anchor. One day, to its horror, it lost its anchor and drifted into open waters. When knocked around by stormy seas it asked some other boats for help. They replied, "Remain in the open sea until you understand it."

The boat fought the advice at first, but finally succeeded in seeing that the open sea was its true home. Fear vanished.

Later, it met a new boat from the harbor which had just lost its anchor. The terrified boat asked, "Do you know how to help me?"

"Yes, I know," the older boat replied, then added with a sigh, "I also know how you will fight everything I tell you."

The loss of psychological anchors, such as dependency and self-centered thought, can be wisely used to enter the whole of life.

THE DECEIVER

There was once a man with a compulsive need to deceive people, for it gave him a feeling of power and superiority. Feeling ill one day, he went to a doctor who gave him the correct medicine. "Take a spoonful every day," instructed the physician. The man promised to do so.

Every morning the man poured out a spoonful of medicine, and with a broad grin, poured it down the kitchen sink.

Of course, the man grew sicker and sicker every day, until he had to enter a hospital. As the doctor approached, the man silently shouted in triumph, "Ah! Another victim!"

The first deception is self-deception.

THE FEELING OF ANNOYANCE

Said Gerald at class, "I am trying to let these principles work for me in everyday situations. Today, I had an interesting experience. A man took my place on the company parking lot. It annoyed me. What do I need to know?"

"Your real nature was not annoyed at all. The old nature simply loved the feeling of annoyance, for it made you feel important. Under different circumstances you might have felt pleased, for example, had your place been taken by a pretty girl. Don't let a false fondness for annoyance and agitation carry you away from yourself."

Just as you would not let a tornado carry you off, you must not permit stormy emotions to pull you away from yourself.

THE NATURE OF TRUE LOVE

"What is the nature of authentic love?" a class asked the teacher. He replied, "I will give you four explanations. Each connects with another."

The teacher continued, "True love exists only in a person who has seen through and abandoned his artificial surface personality.

"Genuine compassion never demands anything from anyone, for it dwells within its own completeness.

"Real tenderness is above the level of mere words, above shallow sentimentality, above public dramatics.

"True love is part of the lofty individual who never divides the world into opposites, such as *you* and *I*."

Authentic compassion blossoms naturally within those who go all the way with inner transformation.

THE PERPLEXED SWAN

There was once a young swan who became separated from his family by a storm. He felt an inward urge to find and associate with other swans. However, because he failed to look at his own nature, he did not know what kind of a bird he was. On one occasion he saw some hawks, and thinking he might be one of them, he joined the hawks in a raiding party. He barely escaped the guns of some angry farmers.

In turn he thought he was a mockingbird, a peacock, a duck. All imitations brought grief in one form or another. In despair the swan flew to the tree of a wise old owl to ask, "Who am I?"

"Examine yourself," stated the owl, "and you will know. First you must see who you are *not*."

By dropping labels and imitations we finally dwell within the contentment of our real nature.

BE RECEPTIVE TO THESE INSPIRATIONS

1. Freedom from feelings of distress comes by exploring and understanding them.

2. Remember that most negative emotions are concealed, unconscious, so clear awareness of them is the right medicine.

3. The outer storm ceases the moment the inner storm ends, for they are the same storm.

4. Do not be like most men who secretly love conflict and agitation, but love only peace and decency.

5. A right view of life creates right action, and right action produces right feeling.

6. Notice the peculiar fondness of people for sorrow, then refuse absolutely to value sorrow, for it has no value.

7. Make correction where necessary, but never feel guilty for guilt is slavery masquerading as humility.

8. With right inner work your emotions will never be at the mercy of changing circumstances.

9. Never anchor yourself to anything, for only in detachment can you feel what you really want to feel.

10. Authentic love flows freely and naturally, having no demands because it has no insecurities.

Chapter 11

SECRETS FOR WINNING PERSONAL INDEPENDENCE

THE SECRET TUNNEL

A prisoner-of-war camp contained thousands of men. Life for them was dreary and monotonous—for all but one. There was one man who appeared to be much like everyone else, but was quite different inwardly. He possessed an astonishing secret. He knew of an underground tunnel which led under the fence and to liberty. It had been dug many years before by prisoners who had escaped.

This unique man came and went as he pleased. Possessing the secret, he was as free within the camp as he was when outside.

He tried to tell others about the tunnel, but they were so busy complaining of misfortune they could not pay attention.

Those who know the secret way are in the world but are not imprisoned by it.

TWO O'CLOCK

There was once a foolish man who believed himself to be a great philosopher. One day someone asked him, "What

time is it?'' The foolish man answered, "It is two o'clock."
An hour later another man asked for the time, to which the
foolish man replied, "The time is two o'clock." When a
third man asked for the time the foolish man said, "It is
exactly two o'clock."

The foolish man was asked by his wife, "Why do you always say the same thing, regardless of the time of day?"

"Because my clock always says two o'clock."

"But the clock does not work."

"You do not understand," said the foolish man. "The
clock is the authority for my philosophies. In my sincerity
I submit my humble mind to whatever it may say."

*Do not submit yourself to traditional beliefs, for there
is no true authority except your own enlightened mind.*

THE MARKED ROAD

On his way home a traveler went down a road which was
clearly marked with guiding signs. But very often when
coming to a fork in the road he preferred the appearance of
an unmarked road, which he took. He enjoyed the
excitement of the unmarked roads for awhile, but sooner or
later grew tired of them, so he returned to the signs.

After many weary miles he said to himself, "I see my
error. There is *my* way and there is *the* way. I will make
the way *my* way."

*Let your inner teacher call you back from bumpy de-
tours to the main highway.*

THE SLAVE

Some students asked their teacher to tell them of an experience of his with inquirers. The teacher began, "I once
met a slave. Though his slavery was inward, it was just as
binding as if he wore actual chains. When I casually mentioned his plight he reacted as all slaves react. His response
was a combination of disbelief, scorn, bewilderment and
rejection. Had he been receptive, I could have helped him,
for awareness of slavery must precede freedom."

The teacher continued, "What awareness could have helped him? I could have told him he was the slave of everyone he needed to impress, of everyone he feared, of those he depended upon for psychological security. He could have seen his enslavement to shame over past follies, and could have understood how shame prevents understanding and freedom."

The test of a man's teachability is to tell him about his chains and watch how he takes it.

WHAT CLAUDE SAW

A class in California was given a specific assignment. Each member was to carefully observe his own mind in order to see something which needed correction. "Remember a basic rule of mental wholeness," the class was told. "Honest awareness of a negative condition is the first step toward removing it."

Claude reported at the next meeting, "It is not easy for me to come out with it, but I see how most of my reactions are determined by exterior influences. A word or a letter or face tells me what to think, and it is often an unpleasant thought. But having been shocked by seeing this, I also see possibilities I never saw before. I want to be my own influence, which is why these teachings are my great passion in life."

The one sure way to attain self-command is to strive each day for a bit more self-knowledge.

THE APOLOGETIC MAN

There was once a man with a very apologetic nature. He felt compelled to explain everything he did to everyone he met. For instance, when not buying something at a shop he explained to the owner, "But maybe I'll buy something tomorrow."

Not liking his fearful submission, he sought help. He found a book entitled, *EXPLAIN TO NO ONE BUT YOUR-SELF.* The book showed the way to independence from

people and events. It said in part, "Explain your behavior
to yourself until you are aware of hidden motives and desires. This awareness frees you of explanations to others.
Your true nature never apologizes. Does a lion apologize
for being a lion?"

The man felt great relief and never apologized again.

*These principles teach you to be yourself, and that
real self is independent of the criticisms and opinions of
others.*

THE INVISIBLE FENCE

Through a system of rewards and punishments, a collie
was trained by its owner to never leave the yard. Though
there was no fence, the dog never crossed the invisible
boundary line and therefore never knew anything about the
outside world.

Later, a new owner of both the collie and the home tried
to lead the dog through the invisible fence, but it refused
to go. However, through gentle unlearning, the collie was
finally set free.

*Anyone can unlearn his self-limiting ways of thinking
to cross over to the abundant world.*

AUTHENTIC SELF-COMMAND

There was once a man who believed he commanded the
events in his life. He owned a factory in which he had authority over many employees, and he also had a pretty
wife. His relationship with them protected his belief in self-
command.

One day the factory failed and the wife went away. The
man felt he had lost himself. Being a student of esotericism
he asked a teacher for an explanation. He heard, "You believe you possess a separate self. This illusion creates a
second illusion, that is, you think this self can and must
command other people. Give up your false belief in a separate self. This ends the false need to command others,

which ends anxiety also. Then you will be one with yourself, one with life, and will have authentic self-command."

These principles make sense where nothing else does, and that is because they are right.

GOOD AND BAD NEWS

A student of esotericism raced excitedly up to his teacher to exclaim, "I have just heard good news!"

"I am sorry," the teacher replied, "but it is bad news."

The teacher explained to the bewildered student the meaning of the term *identification*. "You call an event good news when you identify with it. This means the event seems to affirm your acquired sense of self, seems to prove your invented identity. Likewise, you say another event is bad news because it seems to threaten this imaginary self."

A week later the student sighed sadly to the teacher, "I have just had bad news."

"No," said the teacher, "it is good news, for now you can better understand identification and get rid of its injury."

Rise above both good and bad news to where every event is met with understanding and self-command.

INFORMATION FOR BETTY

Betty first attended class when having a domestic difficulty, and continued in class when the problem ended. She was often the first to request information, such as this: "Please discuss the need for seeing ourselves as we are, not as we imagine we are."

"You never see yourself when supported by others, whether socially, financially, spiritually. You see your state only when supports collapse. *There* is your great opportunity. Don't miss it! Be aware that you were not standing alone, not thinking for yourself. Pass through the shock and you will reach the door of deliverance. Don't miss it!"

Real change occurs within the person who uses shocks as lessons in self-discernment.

CONVERSATION ABOUT VALUES

Two men fell into a conversation about their philosophies toward life. Said one, "I value the simple virtues of integrity and sincerity. Also, I value books which guide me toward a higher life."

"Very interesting," said the second man, "for that is also what I consider valuable."

The first speaker was unaware of the gulf between his words and his heart. His life was out of control, though few knew it.

After careful self-examination during earlier years, the second man had seen through his shallow ways. This had led him to sincerely value higher truths. He was a self-commander.

There is no way to separate what we actually value from what happens to us, so an investigation of values is wise.

THE ESSENTIAL LESSON

A seeker came to a teacher to say, "Do you remember my visit with you a few years ago? I wanted help in finding the answers to life, so I told you I was attending the lectures of famous and popular scholars. You said very little to me during the visit, and I still do not know why. I have come today to admit to childish thinking. I once believed that a man's fame and popularity indicated inner trueness. I learned only one thing from all those famous men. I learned they do not know."

"To know that was essential," said the teacher. "Now you can be helped."

Run away swiftly from any person or organization offering to take over your own mental responsibilities.

THE FRONT GATE

A man was once put in prison. As the front gate closed

behind him, he had the impression that the guard did not lock it. He said to another prisoner, "I think the gate is unlocked." The other man shook his head. "No, it is secure."

The man asked dozens of other prisoners, but they all said the same thing: "There is no way out. The gate is locked."

But the man's first impression was correct. The gate *was* unlocked so he walked out.

Unhappy man's first impression is correct, for the gate is unlocked, there is a way out.

CLASS IN WISCONSIN

A class in esoteric truth in Wisconsin listed these clues for attaining personal independence:

Gordon: "Strangely, an early sign of self-liberty consists of our dawning awareness that we really do not know what is good for us."

Maxine: "When coming to conclusions, make sure they are your own, and not merely borrowed."

Stanley: "What keeps a man chained is his refusal to accept the humiliation of seeing that his present position is all wrong."

Lola: "The next time you feel that someone or something stands in the way of what you want, ask how you would feel if you no longer wanted it."

Vincent: "If you have to get involved in something, get involved with your psychological independence."

Right now, as you hold this book, the path to freedom starts right in front of you.

THE REASON WHY

A teacher gave a public lecture which was attended by many people who had not heard higher truths before. The teacher stressed the theme, "It is your life. You can do whatever you want with it. For good or bad, it is entirely up to you."

Afterward, the teacher's regular students asked why he had stressed that theme. He explained, "It arouses a number of responses which can be favorable to anyone with anything worthwhile inside. It cuts away his belief that others can or should rescue him, thus encouraging self-responsibility. It challenges his false assumption that he is a helpless victim of circumstances, which in turn challenges self-pity. It throws him on himself, makes him feel all alone. If he *uses* this critical moment wisely, instead of fearing it, he admits a ray of psychic sunshine."

Self-reliance is a cosmic law, which means that the only person who can solve a problem is the person having the problem.

THE SELF-COMMANDING KING

There was once a king whose empire stretched from sea to sea. But with all his wealth and power he felt empty within. Turning to spiritual studies, he finally attained what he really wanted—self-command.

One day the king told a close friend about his inner adventures. "Others would not understand all this," the monarch explained, "but I know you do."

The friend asked, "What caused the turning point?"

The king replied, "When I saw the real ruler of the land. Let me show you what people really worship."

The king reached out and held up the royal uniform.

If you want the command which is above men, do not seek it in the ways of men.

THE POISED TEACHER

A new student and an advanced disciple were discussing their teacher. "He is a marvel of poise and judgment," praised the new student. "How superbly he handles questions from the audience, even when some of the questions are foolish or pointless. Is it possible," asked the student, "for me to attain this perfect command?"

"Of course."

"When will it happen?"

"When you are awake to what is awake in you."

An awakened man is like a captain who knows both ship and sea, and who is therefore never upset by a nervous passenger.

THE MAN WHO UNDERSTOOD

There was once a man who understood many things. Truly realizing the beauty in simplicity, he lived quietly and sanely. He had no compulsive ambitions to grab for society's shallow prizes.

One day his neighbor raced over to shout, "Did you hear the awful news? Some people have formed a pressure group to serve their own selfish interests. But this means the end of our own benefits. Help me organize our own pressure group to fight back. Do you see what I am trying to do?"

"Yes," replied the hearer. "I see that you have a problem, and wish to convince me that it is also my problem. Pardon me, but I am not part of the madness."

A man with true insight never permits society's violence to intrude upon his sanity.

THE CHAINS

There was once a citizen of a certain country who moved about awkwardly and uncomfortably. This was because his arms and legs were bound with chains. But because he never questioned his bondage he became quite used to it. In fact, had anyone told him about his chains he would have denied having them at all. This was because he and everyone else gave their chains fancy names, such as "Jewels of Freedom" and "Ornaments of Honor."

One day the chains made him especially uncomfortable, which made him aware of them for the first time. Though shocked, he took an even closer look. To his delight and astonishment he saw that the chains were made of paper, not of steel as he had first supposed. So he broke the paper chains and moved freely about ever after.

Chains of unhappiness can be broken by seeing that they have no real power.

TRUE INDEPENDENCE

The topic of individual independence was introduced by Louis in an afternoon class. He said, "People love to preach about human independence, but have you ever studied the distorted faces of those who scream about liberty? You can see they are slaves to themselves. Please discuss true independence."

"Independence is individual, never collective. You must begin to stand alone in order to see that you are not really alone. You see you are not alone because you also see you are not a separate ego which is apart from the Universe. Strangely, man says he wants independence, but refuses the true independence found by ending the false independence of the ego-self. You will know true independence when your nature and Universal Nature are One, which they are in reality."

Think of independence as being a state of freedom from whatever is inwardly wrong, for that is the true and the only independence.

THE WILD MAN

There was once a man whose life ran wild. He was a near-alcoholic, he eventually fought with everyone he met, and he was tormented daily by violent thoughts.

Someone told him about a true teacher who knew the cause and the cure of human ruin. "You understand," the wild man was told, "that you must listen carefully to what he says about finding a new life. Then you must energetically turn the words into right actions."

The wild man exploded with anger and indignation. "Are you mad?" he roared. "I must learn about a new life? What? And lose control of my own life!"

The more a man is out of control the louder will he insist that he possesses self-control.

THE TOPAZ

While on a stroll, a student of esotericism found a stone he believed to be a topaz. Knowing his teacher was a gem expert, he brought the stone to school to ask, "Is this a genuine topaz?"

The teacher instructed, "Go to the library and read everything there about the topaz." The student departed, returning an hour later to say he had followed instructions.

The teacher said, "I can now tell you that the stone in your hand is a genuine topaz."

Asked the student, "Is there some reason you did not tell me that before?"

"Yes. I have taught you and the others many times to not be gullible. Test everything personally. You can now match what I told you with your own discoveries. Whether with gems or with life, you are quite capable of being your own expert."

No one knows the truth better than you, provided you know what it means to live with the true you.

KEY TO THE KINGDOM

A weary wanderer met a stranger who told him, "At the end of this road is a peaceful kingdom. There is a gate at its entrance which requires a key. Somewhere along the road you will find the key."

After many days of travel the man reached the gate. To his surprise, the gate was open, so he walked in. Sighting the stranger again he said, "I am very grateful to you, but why did you mention a key when the gate was already open?"

The stranger replied, "People always think in terms of the known and the familiar, but the key is different from what they think. The key was your own persistent wish for the kingdom."

When you think of freedom, think of freedom from your own misunderstandings, for that is right thinking.

THE INNOCENT JEWELER

In Germany many years ago a powerful baron possessed a ring he prized highly. One day he gave it to his jeweler to be polished. But one night some enemies of the baron stole the ring and hid it in their own quarters. When the anxious jeweler reported the theft to the baron's guards, he was imprisoned. The jeweler tried to explain his innocence, but his own fear and confusion made his story seem false.

While seated in his cell, the jeweler put his mind to work. Remembering the baron's enemies, and his own carelessness, he realized what had happened. He requested a few minutes with the baron, which was granted. As a result, the ring was recovered and the jeweler was set free and restored to his former position.

Man's psychological imprisonment is a result of a gigantic misunderstanding, a cunning hoax, but a hoax he can expose.

FOLLOW THESE PATHS TO PERSONAL FREEDOM

1. One part of you is entirely independent of society's confusion, so make it your task to awaken it.

2. Constantly call yourself back to yourself, for each effort weakens the grip of psychic tyranny.

3. Your very willingness to hear about your mental chains is the unlocking key.

4. Correct learning consists largely of unlearning wrong attitudes and acts.

5. When something really makes sense you feel it, which is why these principles are increasingly attractive.

6. Build spiritual integrity by seeing whether an offered idea agrees with your own deep sense of rightness.

7. Liberty exists, freedom is ahead, there is a way out, so march ahead in spite of everything.

8. True independence ends gullibility, which means that the free man is never deceived or hurt by other people.

9. Think of freedom as an inward attainment, never as something to be gained from the outer world.

10. Remind yourself over and over that the prison of unhappiness has no bars except incorrect thoughts.

Chapter 12

A TREASURY OF METHODS
FOR SELF-ELEVATION

THE ELM TREE

A teacher of natural science told a new class, "The word I wish you to remember is *investigation*. If you wish to discover the secrets of science, let that word guide you."

The teacher then invited the students to look out the school window to the yard below, which they did. "Observe that large elm tree," said the teacher. "It has a secret which investigation will reveal. It sounds incredible, but the leaves of that tree exhale several *tons* of water every day. The point is, use personal investigation to make a natural fact your fact. Otherwise, you will not know but will not know that you do not know."

Be scientific in self-investigation, which means you wish to find what is there, not what you hope is there.

OLD WORLD AND NEW WORLD

Said a seeker to a teacher, "I wish to leave the Old World and enter the New World."

"To do this," the teacher answered, "you must see where the Old World exists."

159

"Where does it exist?"

"Nowhere but in a wrongly-operating mind, a mind living in the illusion of time. As an aid to beginners we sometimes use the words *Old World* and *New World*, but these are mere labels arising from the level of conditioned thought. You must eventually rise above both the Old World and the New World."

"Then what will there be?"

"One World."

Your mind creates the kind of world you inhabit, so uplift your mind and you rise to a higher world.

THE NEW FRUIT

Through skillful crossbreeding a great botanist created a new kind of fruit. Its taste was far superior to any other fruit in existence. The botanist offered a taste of the fruit to three of his neighbors. Each neighbor, who had his own favorite fruit, gave a reason for refusing the unique fruit.

"It has no resemblance to an apple."

"Oranges are good enough for me."

"I'm afraid it won't taste like a peach."

From that day forward the botanist offered his new fruit only to those who could think outside of their past.

To taste a totally different kind of life, dare to detach yourself from the familiar and the habitual.

HIGHER CONSCIOUSNESS

"You have emphasized the need," said Robert, "for abandoning habitual thought in favor of higher consciousness. Please discuss this."

"You must not abandon habitual thought in everyday matters, otherwise you would not remember how to drive your car. But you must uncover and end all thoughts about who you are, about your supposed identity. Without self-thought there is no sense of identity. But this is so frightening to most people—falsely frightening—they refuse to let go of what they call themselves. But the end of the false self is the beginning of wholeness. When self-labels disappear your day alternates between practical thought, as when gardening, and consciousness, in which there is no fixed and frightened self."

See the difference between wrong thought which includes self-labels, and higher consciousness, which is free of nervous self-references.

THE BEWILDERED METAL

A strip of metal once rested comfortably on a low shelf in a factory. It remained there for a long time, doing nothing but collecting dust.

One day a workman picked it up, carried it to a bench, and began to twist it out of its usual shape. "Why are you doing this to me?" shouted the alarmed and frightened strip of metal.

"To enable you to see wonders beyond your imagination," replied the workman. "Just now it all seems strange and frightening, but someday you will be very glad. You see, I am turning you into a telescope."

A willingness to pass through inner change enables us to see the vastness beyond our present position.

SHEEP IN THE PASTURE

Two sheep were discussing human beings. "People are peculiar," commented one sheep, "including our owners."

"Why do you say that?" inquired the other.

"Well, look. They spend lots of money getting this fine pasture into shape, then spent several weeks putting a fence around it. Then what do they do? They go and live in a house."

A man's viewpoint is the only one he thinks is logical.

AT THE KING'S COMMAND

Several hundred years ago a French king ordered the

construction of a canal. It ran from a distant river to the interior of the castle.

One summer an enemy army surrounded the castle, cutting off the water from the canal. The defenders of the castle grew increasingly worried as the water supply ran low. Talk of surrender spread around the castle. On a day when the situation seemed hopeless, the king ordered everyone to assemble in the courtyard. At the king's command, some soldiers lifted a covering on the ground to expose a secret well. "There is ample water here," announced the king, "which the enemy cannot touch."

Finally realizing that the castle had an inner supply of water, the enemy departed in defeat.

Since no one can successfully attack the truth, our oneness with truth insures our safety.

THE MAN WHO SOUGHT TRUTH

A man who wanted help in straightening out his life asked a teacher, "Do you know the truth?"

Replied the teacher, "Please do not be gullible. How can you know whether I know the truth unless you know at least a bit of it yourself? If a man talks about farming only a farmer knows whether the man states the truth or not."

"But how can I know in order to know whether or not you know?"

"Come here every day with a truly receptive mind."

Receptivity to the truth and to the truth alone is a wise way to locate an authentic source of higher guidance.

A TRICK OF THE MIND

Joyce commented, "I have observed that many people feel cheated by life, which possibly includes me. How can we end this self-damaging attitude?"

"Work with this concise answer. The denial of his desires is not what really bothers a man. That is just a cunning trick of the mind. He deliberately manufactures ways to feel cheated in order to thrill at the fiery indignation it arouses. This strong feeling seems to confirm his illusion of having a separate ego, for complaint seems to create a complainer. It is this illusion of a separate self which he falsely treasures above all else."

Command of the mind begins with an understanding of its wrong ways.

GOOD AND BAD

A man asked a teacher, "What does it mean to be either good or bad?"

Asked the teacher, "How do you judge whether another man is good or bad?"

"If he agrees with me, he is good, if not, he is bad."

"Ah! So that is your entire system of morality! You do not see his goodness or badness; you judge him by your own *ideas* about good and bad. So you are not really concerned with morality; you are concerned with yourself. Believe me, true goodness is much higher than that."

Authentic goodness dwells in those who have transcended personal opinions about good and bad.

CARROTS AND RADISHES

A citizen wanted to grow some carrots, so he consulted a man who was known as the Famous Gardener. Buying some seeds from the Famous Gardener, the man planted them. A few weeks later he proudly invited a friend, "See my fine carrots!"

"*Carrots?*" exploded the staring friend. "These are *radishes!*"

"Impossible. The Famous Gardener said they were carrots. Who are you to question his great authority?"

"You can call them carrots," said the friend, "but they will remain radishes. How strange that you refuse to see this, even after tasting them. Do you know when you will get carrots? When you really want carrots."

*We can begin to grow the right products by frankly ad-
mitting that we are not presently growing them.*

THE THREE BARRIERS

"There are three major barriers to your progress," an
advanced student of esotericism told some new pupils.

"Just three!" burst out a listener. "Please tell us what
they are and how we can conquer them."

Replied the advanced student, "Ask daily whether you
might be thinking that something is true which may be
quite untrue."

"And the second?"

"Never shield yourself from criticism."

"The third?"

"Get over the thought that you have just three barriers
to your progress."

*It is positive, not negative, to see how many barriers
we must hurdle, for it is a part of healthy self-honesty.*

THE DECORATED HALL

A teacher had a special method for separating the
merely curious from those who yearned for real wisdom.
He let his assistant occupy a large lecture hall, richly decorated and attractive to the eye. The teacher himself remained in a small and plain room a block away.

All inquirers were first directed to the assistant, who
taught them many truths. But occasionally he hinted that
higher wisdom could be found in the plain room down the
street.

There were always more people in the decorated hall
than in the plain room.

*Wisdom for self-transformation resides on a level
much higher than habitual eyes can see.*

SELF-ADVANCING STATEMENTS

Members of a study group in Florida supplied these self-
advancing statements to new students in the group.

Walter: "There is no law which compels yesterday's blunders to repeat themselves today, so your adventure is to experience this present liberty."

Evelyn: "The next time you want self-promotion, promote the idea that mental stillness and true power are the same thing."

Patrick: "Do not assume that understanding the words about the truth is the same as living within the truth."

Clyde: "Spiritual law can never be against you, for *you are* the law, which means that in reality you are not divided against yourself."

Virginia: "Never hesitate to travel a long way in search of truth, for what other really important task do we have?"

For today's project, develop and write down several self-advancing statements, then think about them.

THE AWARD

There was once a dissatisfied man who believed he would be happy by obtaining more money. Several schemes for getting rich ended in nothing. One day he read a news item which filled him with fresh hope and excitement. The story told about a medical scientist who had been given an international award for his great discoveries in human health. The award included a large sum of money.

The dissatisfied man sought out the scientist to ask questions about his success. The scientist began to tell about his many years of patient research. He was soon interrupted by the dissatisfied man who exclaimed, "Never mind the details. When do they give the next award?"

People want to separate happiness from patient self-study, which is like trying to separate a violin from its own music.

HUMAN HYPOCRISY

Two friends were discussing a teacher of higher thought. "I have heard him lecture," said the first man, "and I can tell you that he sees human beings as they really are, not as they pretend to be."

The second man expressed interest in hearing the teacher, but was told, "Not everyone is ready for such honest revelations. We must see our own faults, and not just find fault with others. However, you can accompany me to the next lecture. Your own reaction will determine whether you are ready to find yourself."

After the first lecture, the second man exclaimed, "How right you are! That man sees straight through human hypocrisy!"

"What makes you say that?"

"He described several people I know!"

Seeing ourselves as we really are may be surprising, but nothing is more healthy.

THE SIX WITNESSES

A teacher told this story: "Six men journeyed toward a magnificent temple which none had ever seen. Three of them stopped a mile away from it, while the other three stopped a half-mile away.

"When returning home, all six men described the temple to their friends. The loudest and most authoritative were those who remained a mile away."

The teacher concluded, "The greater the distance between a man and the truth, the more he deceives himself into believing he understands it. So take care to whom you listen."

These truths supply a new kind of confidence in which you listen not to human error, but to your own purified nature.

DECEIVED DORIS

Doris opened a class discussion in Iowa by saying, "Without mentioning details, I was deceived by someone I trusted. It was my own fault, I know, but how can I prevent future hurts?"

"Would you like to know the actual root of the pain?"

"Yes, please."

"And will you think about it for the next few days?"

"Yes."

"It was shame over your own gullibility. You had a self-image of being alert and wise. Getting deceived smashed this image, causing shock and resentment. Let the image remain smashed, for that makes room for sharp insight. Then, that kind of pain will not repeat itself because you will recognize a deceiver when you see one."

Nothing is more protective in daily affairs than a clear mind, a mind free of harmful images.

BIRD IN THE BUSH

Two students paused in a journey to rest beneath a tree. Their attention was attracted by a small bird perched on a bush a short distance away. One of the students suddenly shouted and waved his arms, at which the bird darted away.

In surprise, his companion asked, "Why frighten a harmless bird?"

The other man sighed. "That is how we all misunderstand. I saved that bird from a hawk you did not see."

We misunderstand life's lessons, taking them as harsh treatment, when they are really our rescuers.

HOW PAIN VANISHES

A bewildered man complained to a teacher, "Whichever way I turn in life I get hurt."

Asked the teacher, "Who is this self that gets hurt? Describe this person you call *yourself*."

The man supplied his name, his occupation and other details.

"But you are none of these things," informed the teacher. "These are simply acquired words and ideas about yourself. Get rid of them and pain will vanish."

"But all this is so mysterious. I don't understand."

"Do you really want to understand?"

"Yes."

"Then come here regularly until you do."

Remember the importance of discovering who you are not, for then you will know who you are.

THE ENTERTAINER

Reaching a fork in the road, a party of travelers did not know which turn to take. Their attention was attracted by a nearby entertainer who performed a clever singing-and-dancing act. The travelers were so amused they forgot they were on the road. Sitting down, they applauded the entertainer and gave him money.

Also nearby was a man who simply pointed out the correct turn to anyone who came over and asked.

An authentic teacher never says anything to merely entertain or stimulate anyone, but speaks only to instruct.

THE CURE FOR ANXIETY

Asked Harold, "What is the basic cause of anxiety?"

"A person unconsciously labels himself as Man A, that is, he calls himself a success or anything else which seems to provide individuality. This creates the opposite of Man B, for A cannot exist without B. But now A is anxious, for anything opposite to his label becomes an enemy or competitor."

"So how does anxiety end?"

"By not creating the illusion of being Man A. If A ends, B also ends. But a man fears to drop his label of being A because he thinks it steals what he calls his individuality. Also, he cannot conceive a state which is above all labels, above both A and B. But this free state exists. You are here in class to find it."

Understand that you neither have nor need a self which must hold the world together—and you will be in the World.

THE CHOICE

A duke in earlier days in England needed a reliable horseman to carry messages from his estate to London. Two soldiers requested the appointment. "The better man will qualify himself," said the duke. "Both of you will ride for a few weeks. Do not make unnecessary stops."

At the end of several weeks, the duke was ready to decide. In turn, he rode each of the soldier's horses to London. He observed a difference in the habits of the two horses. One of them slowed down or stopped at almost every inn along the way. The other horse kept a steady forward pace.

The duke knew which rider to choose.

Our daily habits are better clues to our actual nature than our words.

FIVE VITAL FACTS

Five students asked their teacher to give them the single most vital fact each needed to know. The teacher addressed each learner in turn:

"Know that you never suffer from anyone but yourself."

"Realize the existence of higher points of view."

"Understand that sentimentality is not love."

"See that you are not the person you assume you are."

"Perceive that the truth's only aim is to cure."

Discover something which is vital for you to know, then concentrate your attention toward understanding it.

THE STRANGE ROAD

A mountain road in the state of Montana was used regularly by tourists. Their destination was the peak of the mountain which offered a spectacular view of the forest below. Every once in a while the road seemed to object to its use, for it collapsed in certain sections, leaving impassable pits. The road required so much repair the local authorities began to examine it. For several weeks they found no explanation for the road's tendency to destroy itself.

One investigator decided to search through some old records of the area, which revealed the cause of the strange pits. Certain stretches of the road had been built over copper mines which had been abandoned many years earlier.

A new road was built over solid ground.

You are building a new road through life, a road having no mental or emotional pits.

IMPORTANT INSTRUCTIONS TO REMEMBER

1. Investigate these ideas with a passionate wish to discover what life is all about.

2. Ordinary thinking has its place in daily affairs, but let your whole life be under the guidance of your whole mind.

3. Have no apprehension when reality places you in unfamiliar circumstances, for your whole mind commands all circumstances.

4. A truly receptive mind is like the dawn which eventually reveals a magnificent world.

5. A man who does not like the taste he is getting from life needs only to change his spiritual food.

6. Nothing compels anyone to repeat his blunders except his own mechanical thinking, which consciousness can correct.

7. Write down a guiding idea which appeals to you, then put it into action for the next few days.

8. Authentic confidence is effortless, for it arises naturally from a life united with cosmic power.

9. The only purpose of truth is to help the individual, to cure him of everything needing cure.

10. The reason why you should proceed with good cheer is because nothing is more delightful than the upward journey.

Chapter 13

SPECIAL GUIDANCE FROM ESOTERIC SCIENCE

THE LAW OF CAUSE AND EFFECT

In frontier days of America, several gold prospectors camped alongside a river. They cut down a dozen trees to use as logs for a cabin. But in a sudden change of plans they abandoned their camp in favor of a new site several miles downstream.

One day, after a heavy rain, they were panning gold in the swollen and rushing river. Suddenly, an alarm was shouted. The men looked up to see several logs hurtling down the river toward them. Struggling frantically, they barely made it out of the way in time.

One of the frightened men gasped, "The rising river carried those logs down here. They are the ones we ourselves cut."

By the law of cause and effect, we ourselves put into motion the events we experience.

THREE ANSWERS

The following exchange took place between teacher and inquirer: "How can I avoid a noisy world?"

"Be quiet yourself."

"How can I avoid getting hurt?"
"Be harmless yourself."
"How can I avoid false teachings?"
"Be true yourself."
Whatever kind of psychological events a man meets, he really meets himself, for he and his world are one.

GEORGE AND LUCY

George and his wife Lucy stayed after class to say, "You state that we are our own psychological atmosphere, for good or bad. May we hear more?"

"Smile and frown into a mirror. Are those states in the mirror, outside you? No, they are within. What you *see* you *are*, so at all times you are your own atmosphere. This is difficult for people to see, mainly because they do not want to see it. Blaming someone else is easier. Even if another person frowns at you it can have no effect unless you also occupy his negative atmosphere. Change yourself and you change your atmosphere, for they are exactly the same."

Good things happen when a man sees that he has no life-atmosphere except the one he creates for himself.

THE MAN WHO WAS RIGHT

Three friends were seated on an outdoor bench. Two of them were having a lively argument over religion and philosophy. Each accused the other of being childish and superstitious. They finally turned to the third man to say, "You heard everything. Who is right?"

Replied the third man, "You would never believe me if I told you."

"Tell us anyway."

"*I* am right."

"What do you mean?"

"I don't have to convince you I'm right."

The man who really knows has no compulsion to prove it.

THE GLEAM IN THE STREAM

An inquirer called upon a wise man whose cabin was located in the center of a broad meadow. As they stood outside the inquirer lamented, "I look everywhere, but cannot see truth."

"The gleam of a sunny stream can be seen from here," stated the wise man. "Turn and look in several directions."

The inquirer followed instructions, but failed to see the stream.

"There is one precise direction in which you did not look," the wise man said. "Find it and look that way."

With diligent action the inquirer found the right direction and saw the gleam of the stream.

Taught the wise man, "Willingly exhaust your wrong viewpoints, after which you will look in the right direction."

This way is true magic, for with it you are able to see what was formerly invisible.

TELEVISION NEWS

Four people sat in front of a television set and watched a news story. The story was a combination of human madness and human tragedy.

One viewer worried, "I wonder how this event will affect my business?"

A second man accused, "People like that always cause trouble."

The third viewer arrogantly stated, "If people would only listen to my solutions there would be no more such disasters."

The fourth man reflected to himself, "Esoteric science explains why this event happened as it did. There is no mass cure, but thank heaven for individual healing."

The only mind capable of understanding human events is a mind which has transcended its own self-centered errors.

THE PERSECUTED MAN

A distressed man asked a teacher, "Why do people persecute me?"

"Because you ask for it."

"I don't believe that. Explain."

"Without the excitement of persecution you feel you are nothing. When attacked you feel you are at least important enough to be persecuted. Give up your fondness for false excitement and persecution will end. Esoteric science explains all this perfectly."

The law of cause and effect operates unceasingly in human relations, but we can rise above it to dwell in tranquility.

HOW THE WORLD BECAME RIGHT

A boy was given a large map of the world, which he studied and enjoyed. While outdoors one morning his small sister tore the map into pieces. The boy's mother called him inside to explain what had happened to his map. Going to work at once, the boy quickly pasted the map together again.

"How did you put it together so fast?" asked his curious mother.

"It was easy," the boy explained. "There was a map of a man on the other side. By putting the man together the world became right."

When a man is right his world is right, for a man and his world are one.

THE STONES

A group of men were traveling through a rugged land. Having neglected to carry adequate supplies they found themselves without food for lunch. Deciding to rest for awhile anyway, they amused themselves by tossing stones over a row of tall bushes. Tiring of the game, one of the men

climbed a nearby hill. Looking down to the other side of
the bushes, he gasped at what he saw. The tossed stones
were striking a wild pear tree, knocking down and injuring
its fruit.

"Stop throwing stones!" he called down.

"Why stop?" they called back.

"Because I can see the consequences!"

*The ability to see injurious consequences, and thus pre-
vent them, is a unique talent of an awakened man.*

SIGNS OF A STORM

Mr. and Mrs. W. came for a private session. Mr. W. introduced himself, "I am a weather reporter for the government. There are signs of a coming storm, such as changes
in clouds and wind and temperature. Might there also be
signs of an approaching psychological storm?"

"If so," added Mrs. W., "it would help us avoid unhappiness."

"There are many signs you can learn to recognize. One
of them is a demand that events happen according to personal desire. Since events happen by cosmic law, not by individual preference, frustration is inevitable. Another sign
is the seeking of so-called security by joining a group which
believes as you believe. Since this blocks independent
thinking, inner storms are certain."

*Esoteric science enables you to forecast psychological
weather and avoid inner storms.*

THE SADDLE

A man who wanted to buy a fine saddle asked the price.
When told, he waved his arm, shouting, "Too much! Take
off the fancy decorations." When told the new price he complained, "Still too much. Remove something." When given
the third price he scowled, "More than I want to pay. Eliminate something else."

Finally, the man was told, "I hope you are satisfied. The
saddle will cost you nothing."

"Nothing? Wonderful! What do I get?"

"Nothing."

Spiritually, we get according to our willingness to pay, and payment consists of giving up popular but wrong ideas.

PHILIP AND BERNARD

In the days of knights and castles there were two peaceful brothers named Philip and Bernard. Captured by an evil prince, they were imprisoned in separate dungeons.

After a few months, Philip escaped. Then began a difficult adventure to locate and free his brother. Wherever Philip quietly inquired, no one knew anything about Bernard. Turning homeward for a short rest, Philip saw someone entering the family fields at the same time as himself. It was Bernard!

Happily, they exchanged stories. Philip then laughed, "At the same time I was seeking you, you were also seeking me!"

The liberty which the seeker seeks is also seeking the seeker.

THE SHOES

A man was strolling down the boulevard with his wife. Because he was absent-minded he had put on one black shoe and one white shoe.

After a few minutes he turned to scowl at his wife, "Please, dear, try to walk more gracefully. People are staring."

It is much easier to criticize another person than to examine oneself.

THE BROOCH

The day after a shopping tour a woman missed her prized brooch. She told her husband she must have lost it in one of the stores she had visited the day before. She then rushed to the garage to drive back to town. When driving away she thought she heard a shout, but in her hurry and distress she ignored it.

Not finding the brooch in any of the stores, she drove home in a depressed mood. But her face brightened as she saw her husband waiting for her with brooch in hand. "It was behind the sofa all the time," he said. "I called as you drove away, but you moved too fast."

She nodded. "It would have saved lots of grief had I heard."

"I know," her husband said gently, "but yesterday was in the way."

We must cease to listen to our past conditioning, for it prevents hearing the good news found in today.

THE GIFT

A father promised his son a present. An hour later the boy entered the garage and asked for his gift. The father nodded toward a table on which the boy saw some string, sheets of paper, and several strips of wood.

"There is your present," the son was told. Understanding the boy's bewildered stare, the father explained, "I need to put the parts together. Then you will have a soaring kite."

We soar in spiritual skies as we bring our divided nature together into a harmonious whole.

HOW TO HANDLE CHANGE

The second time she attended class, Nancy said, "Most of us dread change. What is the solution?"

"Realize there is no fixed point in you which is apart from change. You are one with change; you are change itself. The will of change is your very own will. Picture yourself in an airplane which changes from east to west, from up to down. Are you apart from the airplane or the changes? No, you and they are the same. Let go of your fixed point. Realize your oneness with change. Dread departs."

Change is never a threat to whoever realizes that he and change are united within the total movement of life.

THE STAIRS

One man was standing at the top of some stairs, while a second man was standing at the bottom. A third man was standing in the middle of the stairs.

The man at the top declared, "These steps go downward."

The man at the bottom stated, "The steps run upward."

"If you were in my position," the third man said to the others, "you would see they run both up and down."

A true view of life includes all viewpoints, not merely the one seen from a presently preferred position.

RAIN

A man often stood at his window and prayed for rain. If the showers came he felt that heaven was on his side. But on dry days he believed he was being punished for his sins.

His neighbor also stood at the window, but he prayed that it would not rain. So in dry weather the neighbor felt favored by heaven. But on rainy days he had bitter feelings of being betrayed by heaven.

There was also a third man who stood at the window. He made no attempt to influence the weather, for he knew it operated on a different cosmic scale than his own. He did not think that heaven was either for him or against him. And he was a sane and calm human being who enjoyed all kinds of weather.

Sanity and enjoyment exist within the man who does not make himself the center of the universe.

INNER TRUENESS IS SUPREME

A seeker was asked by a teacher, "What is two and two?"

"Four."

"Add it so that the answer is five."

"It cannot be done."

"Then make it come out six."

"Also impossible."

"I see. Human error cannot distort the principles of arithmetic. Likewise, inner trueness is immune to attacks from falsehood."

The reason you can win the victory is because truth and health have total power over falsehood and illness.

WHAT HAPPENED TO EVELYN

Evelyn said during an open discussion, "Thirty years ago I attended a social gathering. There I met a person who damaged my life for many years. Why did this happen to me?"

"Had you attended this social gathering in a state of consciousness the event would not have happened. The negative chain of cause and effect would not have started; you would have remained uninvolved. Why? Because consciousness knows human nature as it is, and is never deceived by appearances. When you know an apple is sour you do not eat it. This necessary knowledge of people must start with self-knowledge. Your present is totally free of the past, which we will discuss next time."

The sure way to stop getting hurt by others is to first stop hurting oneself, which comes through self-insight.

THE WINDY LAND

There was a land which was swept by fierce winds all year long. One man, an expert in the ways of the wind, was approached by some people. "Teach us to understand the winds," they pleaded, "so we might build sturdy houses to withstand them."

The expert handed them a book, saying, "This is written in another language. Learn to read it and you will master the wind."

Some replied, "We want help, not work." Others accused, "You put your knowledge into a strange language in order to keep it for your own selfish purposes."

But a few said, "We will learn to read."

The facts a man refuses to investigate are the very facts which can rescue him.

THE FLOATING STICK

While seated by a stream with his teacher a disciple said, "You teach there is a difference between head knowledge and total understanding. What is the difference?"

The teacher took a stick and dropped it to the ground. "That motionless stick is knowledge," he said. Again taking the stick he dropped it into the stream where it briskly floated away.

"That active stick," the teacher continued, "is total understanding. Knowledge can build cities, but by itself it is powerless to carry the inner man forward. Total understanding is a combination of knowledge and flowing essence."

Be willing to rise above accumulated knowledge to the harmony of a whole self.

THE FLOURISHING TREE

Two willow trees grew a short distance from a stream in New Mexico. One of them was sturdy and rich with leaves, while the other was smaller and less attractive.

Over the years the owner of the property wondered why the two trees should have such a different quality and appearance. Unable to find an answer, he dismissed the puzzle from his mind.

One week while digging near the trees his shovel struck something hard. When uncovering it he solved the mystery of the trees. Years earlier, someone had buried large slabs of a stone wall in the spot. The underground wall prevented the roots of the frail tree from reaching the water in the stream. But there was no wall between the flourishing tree and the water.

Blockage of a flourishing life is within, and so is the ability to remove the blockage.

THE COSMIC WHOLE

"We are working on the first floor of the cosmic building," said Gary during an open discussion, "but may we hear something about the ninth or tenth floor?"

"Did it ever occur to you that separate countries do not exist in the eyes of God, of the Cosmic Whole? Whenever you have a name or a label you have separation and therefore conflict. Inasmuch as the Cosmic Whole is not divided in itself it does not divide the world into fragments. Think about this for it connects with your personal life. When you dwell within this Cosmic Whole then *you* do not divide the world into separate countries and peoples. In this state you are whole, unified, and therefore a quiet contributor to social wholeness."

Social healing can come only from those who have first attained individual healing.

THE SYMPHONY

Three friends decided to attend a concert by a famous symphony orchestra. While on their way, each mentioned his favorite musical instrument.

When leaving the concert, one of them remarked, "It would have been a better symphony had they eliminated all instruments except the piano."

Complained the second man, "If only the trumpet had been given a special place."

The third man said, "I would have enjoyed the symphony more had I heard the violin only."

And none of them ever realized what they were really saying.

Since life is a whole and total process, personal preference for one part will prevent our life-harmony.

FACTS ABOUT ESOTERIC SCIENCE

Students in Arizona informed each other of the single most important fact about esoteric science each had learned in the last month:

"I must look at my busy involvements and have the courage to inquire whether I might be hurrying nowhere."

"A person who fails to understand truth will often argue about it or remain silently critical. Both are forms of ego-defense by a frightened person."

"Anything wrong with me will mechanically expand to make things wrong for you, so true morality consists of making myself a right person."

"If you simply drop a fearful thought, where can fear exist? Nowhere."

"Our aim is not to *feel better*, as by changing surface habits, but to *be different* by abandoning artificial personality."

Esoteric science consists of helpful facts and healing changes, available to all.

USE THIS SUMMARY FOR SELF-TRANSFORMATION

1. The man who really sees himself as the cause of his problems will also see himself as his cure, which is a great achievement.

2. The self-unified man is at ease in all conditions, for he has no need to prove himself to anyone.

3. This way enables you to see the invisible, for instance, you grasp instantly the motives and desires of other people.

4. When the man is right his world is right, for a man and his world are the same thing.

5. An awakened man can see trouble before it happens, and thus wisely remain free of it.

6. The kind of life we welcome will come to us, which means we must study what we are welcoming.

7. Let esoteric science explain the mysteries of life to you, for it is able and willing to do so.

8. Truth is supreme, having no opposition and no enemy, so join truth and possess its supremacy.

9. When a man ceases to hurt himself he ceases to be hurt by others, for both hurts are the same inner movement.

10. Your first duty is to save yourself, after which you will know what to do and what not to do toward helping others.

Chapter 14

THE PERFECT PATH TO AN INSPIRING LIFE

OPAL COUNTRY

A man had a deep wish to find some opals. Traveling to a country noted for the gem, he searched around, but discovered nothing. Finally, after several unrewarding days, he found a small opal. The excitement of the discovery surged through and dominated his mind. Though remaining in opal country, he was in a peculiar state of mind. He *searched*, but could not *see*. His mind was so distracted by the small opal he could give attention to nothing else.

An experienced opal-finder came along who recognized immediately the man's strange obsession. The two men talked, after which the obsessed man realized how he had cut himself off from additional opals. "Thank heaven you woke me up," he exclaimed. "I thank you."

We must not fix our minds on a small truth we have found, but must dare to go on to greater discoveries.

HOW THE SOLUTION ARRIVES

"You have stated," said Max in class, "that a deep understanding of the problem will reveal the solution. May we hear more about this?"

"A man lives in terrifying uncertainty, spending most of his time trying to conceal it. He lives in fear because he lacks understanding of liberating cosmic laws. Now in order to understand this he must first be told that he does not already understand. When told this his mind closes like a slammed door. Feeling insulted at being told the truth, he runs away. However, if he were to remain and listen—*even while feeling angry*—he could save himself. By seeing his basic problem, he also sees the solution. When tired of working at something, you don't wonder what to do—you stop working."

Solutions in life are discovered by personal agreement with the truth about life.

THE SAGE AND THE NOBLEMEN

A sage was visited by several noblemen who occupied high places in the kingdom. Each prince or duke was accompanied by a servant who introduced the nobleman to the sage. The sage nodded politely after each introduction, but said nothing.

After giving a short talk about the inward life, the sage left the lecture hall immediately. On the journey home, some of the noblemen complained that the teacher had not shown sufficient respect to their high rank. Grumbled one of them, "He was not even impressed by hearing of my great gifts to the poor."

But one nobleman stated, "You may not return for another lesson, but I will go back very soon. The fact that he was not impressed by us told me another story. I don't trust anyone who is impressed by riches or titles."

To be impressed by the truth itself is the only sensible kind of impression.

THE WANDERING SHIP

In the days of sailing ships, a captain set a course for a port in Ireland. Every evening he carefully charted the next day's journey. After a few days he was bewildered to find that the ship was off course. He checked his calculations every evening, but on the next day he found the ship still heading in the wrong direction.

Only after two weeks was the mystery solved. A stowaway was caught, who confessed to making small but vital changes in the captain's calculations. The stowaway had hoped to reach a port of his own choice.

We must catch psychological stowaways who pull us off course, such as grumbling and self-righteousness.

THE STATE OF AWARENESS

A teacher knew his students did not as yet understand the difference between practical thought and a state of awareness, so he told this story:

"Many years ago an explorer on the island of Bali gave an umbrella to a native, who misunderstood its use. He held it above his head at all times, even in pleasant weather. By doing this he burdened himself unnecessarily.

"Man is like that," explained the teacher. "He fails to see that thought is useful only for everyday tasks, such as conducting business. He tries to use conditioned thought to understand the whole of life, which cannot be done. Only in a state of simple awareness, which is above thought, can he be one with himself and therefore one with all of life. Thought cannot comprehend the whole, for it is but one part of the mind's total function."

Today, begin to see the difference between practical thought and clear awareness, which is whole understanding.

THE NATURAL FLOW OF LIFE

A river once ran through the heart of a certain town. The town was inhabited by agitated people who always needed something to complain about. Looking nervously around, their glance fell on the river. "That river is all wrong," they declared. "We must pass ten-thousand laws to correct it." So they enacted complicated laws and prohibitions about the river. For example, it was ordered to flow slowly on Sunday and to flow swiftly on Monday.

But the laws caused endless conflict. In the one case, half the people demanded a reversal of the law. They wanted the river to flow swiftly on Sunday and slowly on Monday. So from morning to night the people quarreled and hurt each other.

And the river flowed on as it always flowed.

Happy action consists of noninterference with the natural flow of life.

PROTECT YOUR PRIVACY

Bonnie asked, "May we have a simple and clear example of how unawareness causes a problem which consciousness can cure?"

"A woman living in Rhode Island will serve as an example. A few months after starting inner investigation she met some friends she had not seen for three years. The resulting conversation made her uncomfortable. Examining herself, she saw that it was caused by the personal questions the friends had asked about her faltering marriage. She also saw her resentment at their invasion of her private life. But not wishing to offend them, she had answered their questions. Later, she made a decision. At the risk of losing all her friends, she would no longer fear to politely reject any prying into her life. This new awareness ended the problem."

Realizing that familiarity breeds contempt, never permit people to intrude into your personal affairs.

THE GAME-PLAYERS

One day a group of seekers came to an esoteric school to consult the teacher. They were met at the door by an assistant who asked them to remain outdoors for awhile. Somewhat annoyed by this, the visitors looked around for something to do. They noticed a basket by the door which contained several rubber balls. Like gleeful children, they began to play ball games. After awhile they grew tired of games, so very tired that they forgot why they had come to the school. Picking up their coats, they wandered away.

The assistant walked outside and picked up the scattered balls. Sighing, he read once more the message printed on each ball: *WHEN YOU ARE TIRED OF PLAYING GAMES, PLEASE COME INSIDE.* But it was an invitation the game-players never noticed.

The door to newness is not open to those who play at success and popularity, but opens to those who no longer want to play the game.

AT THE AUCTION

Two friends attended a livestock auction where a prize-winning ram was on sale. A magnificent animal, it was eagerly desired by the dozens of people at the auction. The bidding began, and the price of the ram went up and up. Though paying a high price, one of the friends finally obtained the prize-winning animal. He was congratulated enthusiastically by everyone. Smiling, he thanked the people for their good wishes.

As the two friends walked home, they became silent and serious. The new owner of the ram suddenly said to his friend, "I don't need a ram. What should I do with it?"

A person who sees through his false aims and his worthless ambitions is on his way to self-awakening.

WHY MAN IS MISERABLE

"I am unhappy," a man told a sage. "Please help me."

"Tell me a reason for your misery."

"I have failed in my business career."

"Give me another reason."

"I lack the love of a good woman."

"You asked for help," said the sage, "which I will give by explaining you to yourself. The reasons you gave are the inventions of a misunderstanding mind. Not knowing the real reason, you imagine false reasons. Even if you had a thriving career or a good woman you would still suffer anguish. You must see through your own fictions. You are miserable because you are alienated from yourself, because you are split in two. See this."

Explain yourself to yourself, then watch how differently your life unfolds.

AN UNNECESSARY ACT

Asked David, "From the viewpoint of higher logic, what is wrong with trying to impress people favorably?"

"The basic error is assuming you possess a separate self which needs to make impressions. Notice both the thrill of a favorable impression and the pain of failing to make one. Both occupy the same low level of shallow feelings. You want the thrill but not the pain, which is impossible, for they are the opposite sides of the same coin. Your real nature never finds it necessary to make impressions. Study this."

Man creates his own chaos by doing unnecessary things while calling them necessary.

SEEKER AND TEACHER

This dialogue was exchanged between seeker and teacher:

"Can you make me whole?"

"I can show you how to think rightly, after which you will make yourself whole."

"Can you tell me whether to get married or not?"

"I can show you how to know such things from yourself."

"Can you teach me to live in harmony with life?"

"I can teach you to live without ego-interference, for that is the same as living in life-harmony."

"Can you help me understand everything you have said?"

"I can help you develop your own considerable capacity to understand."

Begin your journey now, never hesitating, for you are stronger than all which seems to oppose you.

HOW QUESTIONS END

During a class in Los Angeles a teacher was addressed, "Last week you said there is no answer to a wrong question. Please review this."

"Suppose someone asks you how he can write his name on water. Will you try to answer him or will you point out that the question itself is wrong? Suppose someone asks how he can win over another person. That is a false question because in reality there is no such thing as winning over another; there is only an unhealthy feeling of superiority. But it is very difficult for people to see that their questions make no sense. No man will thank you for exposing his cherished illusions. But you can let insight dissolve pointless questions."

Painful and baffling questions fall away like outworn clothing as our understanding ascends to higher levels.

SLIPS OF PAPER

A school of fish were unhappy with their lives, so they held a conference. "You know," said one of them, "human beings give each other fancy slips of paper which declare that they are qualified and authoritative. By this means they often gain fame and money. Why don't we do likewise?"

So the fish gave each other the fancy slips of paper. But they remained just as unhappy and unwise as before. And the papers did absolutely nothing to protect them from marauding sharks.

"How come," complained one fish, "the fancy slips of paper do good for human beings, but not for us?"

"It does them no good either," stated another fish, "but few human beings know it."

There is only one authority who can bestow life-qualification upon you, and that is your own true nature.

WHERE LOVE EXISTS

Asked Elizabeth, "May we hear more about authentic love?"

"When you say you love someone you really mean that the other person gives you pleasure or a feeling of security. So it is your own feelings which are important, which is certainly not love. Where there is an object of love there is no love; there is only the mind's cunning escape toward an idol. Notice how quickly false love turns into hostility when the object causes displeasure. Where there is an object there is mental division, an illusion that you and the other person are separate beings. Authentic love is above conditioned thought. Love exists in the absence of excited and divisive thought."

True love is the same thing as mental health, psychological wholeness, spiritual trueness.

WHAT THE LECTURER SAW

Two friends came together to hear a lecture about authentic esotericism. One of them came because he had felt a faint but sincere urge to change his life. The other came out of idle curiosity.

The sincere man listened to many disturbing ideas, but he thrilled over their rightness. The idle listener was equally disturbed, but he reacted with hidden hostility.

On the way home the idler attacked the speaker and his message. Feeling personally threatened by the truth, he had no conscience in damaging the budding rightness of his friend. Being weak, the sincere man was half persuaded to not attend additional lectures.

The lecturer himself knew what had happened, for he had witnessed it many times before. He reflected, "One must not be persuaded by evil counselors."

To accept dark advice from those who prefer to ruin themselves is to accept their ruin as your own.

THE SPECIAL COLOR

An artist wished to mix up a special shade of color for his painting of a seacoast. After several experiments he found what he wanted, which was a variety of orange. He set the special color in a separate dish.

He paused in his work to receive several visitors who claimed to posses artistic skill. The visitors examined and criticized the artist's special color, declaring they could give him something far better. So each created a mixture which distorted the artist's original and special color.

As the visitors departed, the artist studied their mixtures. He knew they were all wrong for him. He returned to his own special color and knew it was just right.

Man's illusions and vanities distort the truth, but any individual can find it within his own recovered essence.

TO THOSE WHO GO AWAY

A lecturer gave a series of talks on esotericism. On the last night he told his audience, "I wish to say a few words to those of you who go away, who do not continue with these studies. You fall away because you are not presently ready. This is not said as criticism, but as helpful information. You lose interest because you believe it is too hard to understand. Or maybe your habitual ways feel threatened by the newness of what you have heard. If you only knew that what you fearfully refuse is what you have been seeking all your lives.

"Someday," concluded the speaker, "if the pain becomes unbearable, a distant bell may ring and you will remember what you heard tonight. Then you may wish to return."

Human beings may depart from the truth, still, a total welcome awaits those who wish to return to what is true.

THE STROLLER

A man was strolling down the street with a dog at his side. Suddenly, three people ran out of their homes to block his path.

"Last week your dog chased my cat up a tree," one of the men angrily accused. "I'm not going to stand for it!"

"And why don't you feed him properly?" asked a woman with a self-righteous manner. "He is plainly underfed."

"Yesterday," howled another man, "your dog's barking kept me awake all night."

The stroller quietly replied, "Do you have a need to be so unkind? This dog sensed my friendliness toward him and began to follow me. It is not my dog."

The attacks of foolish people are meaningless to the truly innocent person.

SOMETHING TRUE

"Simply tell me something that is true," a teacher requested his class in Nebraska. He heard from the students:

Donald: "Seeing that you cannot do something is a wonderful stage, for it is the start of doing something."

Barbara: "Our task is to know better that deeper part of us that knows better."

Harvey: "One moment of pure and present consciousness can end forever the tyranny of forty or fifty years in the past."

Virginia: "There is a way to be in your own life without being anxiously involved with it, which is known as self-freedom."

Kenneth: "If you really want to climb, every experience can be used as an upward step."

Discover some simple truth today, then live within it for the rest of the day.

THE SOCIAL ATMOSPHERE

Some students asked their teacher, "How will we be different when attaining enlightenment?"

"You will not become your atmosphere."

"What does that mean?"

"Place a man in a parade and he becomes the excitement of that parade. Set him in a crowd of hysterical people and the hysteria takes him over. Place him in a so-called spiritual atmosphere and he becomes a so-called spiritual person. Upon enlightenment, there will be something in you which is independent of the social atmosphere. The enlightened man is *himself* at all times, which goes unnoticed, for others wrongly assume that he is as weak as they are."

A free mind is no more influenced by social frenzy than the moon is affected by an earth.,/ wind.

THE NEW STUDENT

A teacher and his disciples were having dinner together. The newest student said to the teacher, "Please sir, I have been here only a month, but already I feel blocked. Every day you serve us the same lessons. You urge us to study our minds, to end self-deception, to exercise unused powers. May we hear something new and different?"

Calling in the cook, the teacher said to him, "Please, sir, every evening you serve us delicious dinners. Each dish is a delightful surprise to the taste. However, all this is getting monotonous. Could we have something different?"

The cook smiled in understanding, as did everyone else, including the new student.

Hearing about Reality is never anything but a delight to a receptive mind which loves Reality.

THE ALERT SENTRY

While riding through wooded hills, an emperor of Saxony became separated from his soldiers. Deciding to return by himself, he turned his horse down the road to the palace. When reaching a bridge he was stopped by a young sentry.

Realizing that he was in riding clothes, the emperor invited the sentry, "Look closely. Do you not recognize my face?"

The sentry shook his head. The emperor explained, "Then let me tell you about yourself. You are one of the new volunteers from Brunswick."

Recognizing the emperor at last, the sentry saluted. The passing emperor commended the sentry for his alertness.

Recognize the royalty of truth, then let it proceed to reign in the inner kingdom.

SPECIAL METHODS FOR DAILY PROGRESS

1. Make daring your way of life, for then you will make new and valuable discoveries every hour.

2. Self-transformation occurs by the intelligent process of agreeing with nothing but the truth.

3. Be alertly watchful of your course, then when necessary, pull yourself back to the right direction.

4. Think deeply about the idea of not interfering with the natural flow of life, then let yourself flow.

5. If you are tired of playing the social game, that is good, for now you can learn how to stop playing.

6. Your deeper nature knows all the worthwhile aims you should have, so release these revelations.

7. Your task is to ask right questions, while the task of truth is to supply right answers, which it will surely do.

8. A free man possesses authentic love, gentleness, decency, spiritual wholeness, mental health, physical relaxation.

9. If you want a new delight, let a truth tell you all about yourself, then watch your delight.

10. Everything of true value exists within the kingdom of heaven, so turn your back on the past and step boldly forward.

About Vernon Howard

 Vernon Howard is a unique teacher who broke through to another world. He sees through the illusion of suffering and fear and loneliness. For many years his popular books and lectures on the inner-life have all centered around the one grand topic: "There is a way out of the human problem and any earnest person can find it."

His books are widely used by doctors, psychologists, clergymen, educators and people from all walks of life. More than seven million grateful readers have experienced the power of Mr. Howard's books, including translations into a number of languages. Vernon Howard's clear insight into human nature and his practical solutions attract thousands of new readers worldwide every year.

Informal study groups of men and women use Mr. Howard's books and listen to his taped lectures. For more information, write today to:

New Life, PO Box 2230, Pine, Arizona 85544

(928) 476-3224
Web: www.anewlife.org
E-mail: info@anewlife.org

Please send us
the names and addresses of friends
who may be interested in these teachings.

Praise for Vernon Howard

"Each parable contains truthful, inspiring and riveting insights into human nature."
—Dr. Terry Roche, M.D.

"The stories and lessons in *Inspire Yourself* make it easy for me to understand these advanced spiritual truths. Vernon Howard's writings are like a cool refreshing drink of water in a dry and thirsty world."
—Rev. Tom Russell

"I've never read anything so high, yet so practical and helpful."
—Dr. Lynne Wooldridge, Ph.D.

"Vernon Howard's books are classics, every one of them. Anyone who is fortunate enough to discover Vernon Howard's writings will experience a dimension of life most people only dream of. Do as I have—invest in all of the Vernon Howard classics, then treasure them."
—Bob Proctor, International Speaker